THE THEORY OF KNOWLEDGE

D1304384

BY THE SAME AUTHOR

Materialism and the Dialectical Method
Historical Materialism
Science and Idealism
In Defense of Philosophy

The Theory of Knowledge

By *MAURICE CORNFORTH*

INTERNATIONAL PUBLISHERS, NEW YORK

COPYRIGHT, 1955, BY

INTERNATIONAL PUBLISHERS CO., Inc.

Printed in the U. S. A.

FOREWORD

THE theory of knowledge[1] is concerned with questions about ideas—their source, the way they reflect reality, the way they are tested and developed, their role in social life. These questions have always formed an important part of philosophy.

In bourgeois philosophy the theory of knowledge has come to occupy the first place, on the grounds that before any philosophical conclusions can be drawn about anything whatever we must first make certain of what we really do know and the foundations on which we know it. But bourgeois philosophers have generally approached the subject in the most abstract possible way. Taking nothing else for granted than the bare existence of the individual human mind, they have asked how knowledge could be born and grow up in it. But since human individuals, and still less their minds, do not exist in a void, this kind of inquiry was bound to raise unanswerable questions and to remain comparatively sterile.

Marxism, on the other hand, considers that we ought to study the subject more concretely, and to ask how ideas actually arise, develop and are tested, in the concrete conditions of real human life, in the material life of society. This is why the theory of knowledge is placed not first but last in this series on Marxist philosophy, and why it is introduced only after the discussion of the materialist conception of history.

This volume tries to apply the fundamental ideas of dialectical and historical materialism to show how human consciousness actually arises and develops. It tries to trace this process step by step from its beginnings in the simple conditioned reflex, which is the basic way in which an animal organism enters

[1] Those who consider Greek a more philosophical language than English call it *epistemology*, or sometimes *gnosiology*.

into active relationship with the external world, up to the development of human knowledge and human freedom.

From the conditioned reflex to human freedom—such is the path we shall try to trace.

Approached in this way, the theory of knowledge has both positive and negative significance. Positively, it helps us to evaluate our ideas, to develop them and use them as instruments of human progress. Negatively, it helps us to get rid of all idealism and mystification about the mind of man.

MAURICE CORNFORTH.

London, May 1954.

CONTENTS

Part One

THE NATURE AND ORIGIN OF THE MIND

CHAPTER ONE

MIND AND BODY

The mind is not separable from the body. Mental functions are functions of the brain, which is the organ of the most complicated relations of the animal to the external world. The first form of conscious awareness of things is sensation, which arises from the development of conditioned reflexes.

For the animal, sensations constitute a system of signals of its relations to the external world. In man there has developed a second signal system—speech—which performs an abstracting and generalising function and from which proceeds the entire higher mental life peculiar to man.

Matter and Mind

THE materialist view of the mind is the opposite of the idealist view.

According to idealism, however closely the mind may be connected with its body, it is nevertheless distinct and separable from the body. For idealism, the mind " animates " the body and makes use of the organs of the body both to receive impressions of the external world and to act on the external world ; but its existence does not depend on that of the body. Moreover, idealism holds that while in some of its activities the mind makes use of the body, in other of its activities it does not. For instance, the mind makes use of the body in its sensuous activities, but in its " purer " intellectual or spiritual activities it does not.

This is in essence a very ancient conception. Thus some primitive peoples think of the soul as being a very fine vapour —this is what the word " spirit " originally meant—which resides in the body but which can come out of it and lead an independent existence. For example, the soul journeys out of the body during sleep, issuing forth from the mouth. Again, the

wrong soul can sometimes get into the wrong body—as in
" possession " : a lunatic or an epileptic is said to suffer from an
evil spirit having got into his body. And as part of this primitive
conception of the soul there arises the conception of the survival of the soul after death and also of the pre-existence of the
soul before birth.

Idealist philosophical theories about the mind are, in the
last analysis, only refinements and rationalisations of such
superstitions.

Amongst such refinements and rationalisations is the doctrine
that mind and body are two distinct substances—spiritual
substance and material substance. Material substance, or body,
is extended, has weight, moves about in space. Spiritual substance, or mind, thinks, knows, feels, desires. This view is
still very widely held. It is believed that such properties as
thinking, feeling and so on are so absolutely different from the
properties of matter, that however closely our thinking and
feeling may be bound up with the state of our bodies, they belong
to an immaterial substance, the mind, which is distinct from the
body.

Similarly, idealism, which holds that the mind is separable
from the body, holds that thoughts, feelings and so on are in
no sense products of any material process. If we think and feel
and act intelligently, for example, such behaviour is not to be
explained from the conditions of our material existence but from
the independent functioning of our minds. Admittedly, the mind
makes use of the bodily organs ; but intelligent behaviour stems
from the fact that the body is animated, informed and controlled by an immaterial principle or a spiritual being, the mind.

But such idealist theories, widespread as they are, have long
been offset by opposing materialist views. According to
materialism, so far from mind being separable from body, all
mental functions depend on their appropriate bodily organs
and cannot be exercised without them. All people's conscious
and intelligent activities can be traced back to material causes,
so that far from such activities being exclusive products of mind,
mind itself is a product—the highest product—of matter.

Modern materialism, which is equipped with the results of scientific investigations into the forms of organic life and with the conception of evolution, is able to give a decisive answer to the idealist conception of the mind. Mind is a product of the evolutionary development of life. Living bodies which have reached a certain level of development of the nervous system, such as we find in animals, can and do develop forms of consciousness ; and in the course of evolution this consciousness eventually reaches the stage of thought, the activity of the human brain. The mental functions, from the lowest to the highest, are functions of the body, functions of matter. Mind is a product of matter at a high level of the organisation of matter.

Once this is admitted, there is an end to the conception of the mind or soul as separable from the body and capable of leaving it and surviving it. A mind without a body is an absurdity. Mind does not exist in abstraction from body.

To say that mind does not exist in abstraction from body is not, however, to say that mental processes do not exist or that the mind of man is a myth. Of course, mind, consciousness, thought, will, feeling, sensation and so on are *real*. Materialism does not deny the reality of mind. What materialism does deny is that a thing called " the mind " exists separate from the body. The mind is not a thing, or a substance, distinct from the body.

This point can be illustrated by any example when we ordinarily speak about " the mind ". Philosophers and theologians have imagined that the mind has an existence of its own, and qualities and activities of its own, distinct from the body. But nothing of the sort is ever implied in practical life when we talk about the mind.

Suppose, for example, that you are asked, " What's in your mind ? " This means quite simply, " What are you thinking about ? " In other words, it is a variant of the question, " What are you doing ? " It does not in the least imply that there exists a thing called your mind, distinct from your body.

Similarly, if you are told, " You have a first-rate mind", or " You have a dirty mind", or " You ought to improve your mind", all these remarks are understood as referring to certain things which you normally do. And if you die, or if you are hit on the head or in some other way suffer a disturbance of the brain, then these remarks about your mind no longer apply. For the activities to which they refer can then no longer be performed, since the means of performing them have been destroyed.

A man is endowed with mind, then, in so far as he thinks, feels, desires and so on. But all these activities are activities, functions, of the man, of a material being, an organised body, dependent on appropriate bodily organs. Given a body with the appropriate organisation and the appropriate conditions of life, these activities arise and develop. Destroy the body or its organs, and these activities are destroyed with it. All the mental functions and activities, which are said to be products of mind as distinct from matter, are products of matter. The mind is a product of matter.

Stalin summed it up as follows :

" Thought is a product of matter which in its development has reached a high degree of perfection, namely, of the brain, and the brain is the organ of thought. Therefore one cannot separate thought from matter."[1]

Consciousness and the Nervous System

Not every body is capable of thinking and feeling, but only organic, living bodies. And not every living body manifests those activities which are associated with the development of mind. The appearance of mind is in fact bound up with the evolution of the central nervous system in animals.

When living bodies evolved the nervous system, and when from the central nervous system there developed the brain, then the elementary functions of mind, centring on sensation, came into being. And with the further development of the brain—of the cerebral cortex and its higher centres, which we find in man—there came into being the higher functions of mind, the functions of thought. The brain is the organ

[1] Stalin, *Dialectical and Historical Materialism.*

of thought. Thinking is a function performed by the brain.

Few people nowadays would deny these well-established facts. Nevertheless beliefs are widely held which contradict them. Such, for example, is the belief in personal survival after death. Those who hold this belief usually suppose that in our future conscious existence after death many things will become much clearer to us than they are now. In other words, they believe that our minds cannot attain their full development until after we are dead. They believe that so far from the brain being the organ of thought, our thought will reach perfection only when we have no brain left to think with.

Lenin maintained that in order to arrive at " an analysis and explanation " of mental processes, in order to understand their nature and origin, it was necessary to " set about making a direct study of the material substratum of mental phenomena— the nervous processes ".[1] The foundations of this study have been laid by the work of the great physiologist, Ivan Pavlov.[2] What, then, are the principal conclusions from Pavlov's work which have a bearing on this problem?

Organism and Environment

Before Pavlov, the nervous system was generally regarded as fulfilling the primary function of co-ordinating the action of the different parts of the organism; Sir Charles Sherrington called this " the integrative action of the central nervous system ". Pavlov insisted, however, on the need to investigate " a second immense part of the physiology of the nervous system ". For he regarded it as " a system which primarily establishes the relation, not between the individual parts of the organism, with which we have been mainly concerned hitherto, but between the organism and its surroundings."

The primary function of the central nervous system is not simply to regulate the functioning of the different parts of

[1] Lenin, *What the Friends of the People Are, etc.*, Part I.
[2] See *Scientific Session on the Physiological Teachings of I. P. Pavlov*, Moscow, 1951.

the organism in relation to one another, but to regulate the functioning of the organism as a whole in relation to its surroundings.

Through the functioning of its nervous system, the animal in the course of its activity builds up most complicated relations with its environment, thanks to which it is able to live in its environment, to obtain its requirements and to react to definite conditions in a definite way. Thus the animal relates itself to its surroundings in such a way that it is actively aware of its surroundings, reacts appropriately to events, and in turn acts back upon them. To do all this, the animal uses its sense organs and its limbs, and the organ controlling the whole process is the brain.

The simplest sort of reflex, whereby a stimulus affecting the sense organs evokes a muscular response, constitutes a relation or connection between the animal and its environment. Such and such a stimulus evokes such and such a response—this describes an active relationship of the animal with its surroundings. Pavlov showed that the active relationship of the animal with its surroundings begins from certain fixed and constant connections between the animal and the external world, which he called *unconditioned reflexes*, and develops through the building up of temporary and variable connections, which he called *conditioned reflexes*.

In order to study the development of reflexes, Pavlov used the very familiar fact that animals discharge saliva from the salivary glands in their mouths as a preparation for eating food. Thus a dog presented with food discharges a certain amount of saliva. This is a simple, unconditioned reflex. Present the dog with food, and saliva forms in its mouth. Pavlov then found that if a bell was rung whenever a dog was presented with food, then, after a time, the sound of the bell would itself be sufficient to cause the dog to salivate, even though the food had not yet been presented. This he called a conditioned reflex. For as a result of definite conditions, that is to say, the repeated association of the bell with food, the dog had become conditioned to react to the bell—whereas it never had to be conditioned to react to the food. In other words, the dog had learned to associate the bell with food, and had come to expect food on hearing the bell and so to get ready for the food even before it was actually presented.

Whereas unconditioned reflexes are a part of the heredity of the animal, developed in the course of the evolution of the species, conditioned reflexes are brought into being in the course of the life of the individual—and, having been brought into being, can also be changed or destroyed. Thus if after a time food is no longer presented when the bell rings, then the dog will cease to react to the bell; or it can be taught to react not to any bell but only to a bell of a particular pitch; and so on.

The mechanism of reflexes is found in the brain, in the connections which exist between the sensory and motor centres of the brain. The sensory centres are distinct from the motor centres, the function of the former being to receive messages and of the latter to send messages out. They are connected in such a way that when a message comes in from the sense organs to the sensory centres, it travels across to the motor centres, which then dispatch a message to the muscles, glands, etc.—so that to a given stimulus an appropriate response is made.

An unconditioned reflex is based, then, on a fixed and constant connection which exists between the sensory and motor centres of the brain. And conditioned reflexes are based on temporary, variable and conditioned connections which are formed between the sensory and motor centres in the course of the animal's life.

Such connections between sensory and motor centres within the animal's brain constitute connections between the animal and the external world. For the function of the connections inside the animal's brain is to connect the animal with what lies outside—that is, with its surroundings.

Thus the unconditioned food-saliva connection within the dog's brain connects the dog with its surroundings in such a way that when food is presented the dog gets ready to eat and digest it. And the conditioned bell-saliva connection within the dog's brain connects the dog with its surroundings in such a way that when a bell sounds, which the dog has learned to associate with food, then, once again, the dog gets ready to eat.

An animal lives only by means of its connections with its surroundings, that is, by its external connections which are established through the internal connections within its own brain. Pavlov showed that these connections of the animal with its surroundings are formed through the development of conditioned connections from unconditioned connections, that is, by the development of conditioned reflexes from unconditioned reflexes.

To sum up. An unconditioned connection is a relatively constant, inherited connection between an animal and its environment. If, for instance, something suddenly passes in front of the eye, the eyelids blink : this is an unconditioned connection, which serves to protect the eye. Quite irrespective of the varying conditions which it encounters, the animal relates itself to the surrounding world through such reflexes. It is born with such reflexes, which were formed in the course of the evolution of the species.

A conditioned connection, on the other hand, is a temporary and very variable connection between the animal and its environment, which is acquired by it in the course of its individual life, and which can likewise disappear. A dog, for instance, will go to a certain place for its dinner. This is a connection which it has acquired in the course of its life : it has become conditioned to seek its dinner in that place, in other words, it has learned to seek its dinner there. And if conditions change, then such conditioned connections can be changed correspondingly. The dog can learn to look for its dinner somewhere else.

Pavlov showed that the nervous system of the higher animals has the function of acquiring and establishing temporary and variable connections between the animal and its surroundings, whereby the animal adjusts its reactions to the varying conditions of its environment, and also, by means of its own action on its environment, adjusts its environment to the requirements of the animal.

This function is performed in the brain, and consequently Pavlov called the brain " the organ of the most complicated relations of the animal to the external world".

Activity and Consciousness. Sensations

Pavlov insisted that mental activity is the same as higher nervous activity, and that the different aspects of mental life must be explained by data obtained from the investigation of higher nervous activity. " The dualism which regards the soul and the body as quite separate things is still too firmly ingrained in us", he wrote. " For the scientist, such differentiation is impossible."

Mental activity is an activity of the brain. And if the brain is the organ of the most complicated relations of the animal to the external world, then we must regard mental activity as a part of the activity whereby the animal relates itself to the external world. Its basis is the formation of conditioned reflexes.

Mental life begins when things begin to take on a meaning for the animal, and this happens precisely when the animal, as a result of the formation of conditioned reflexes, begins to learn to connect one thing with another. Something has a meaning for an animal when the animal has learned to connect its presence with something else. For example, a dog learns to connect a particular stimulation of its sense of smell with the presence of some particular food, or of another dog, or of its master, etc., etc. An animal is constantly receiving an enormous number of stimuli through its external and internal sense organs, and it learns to connect the various stimuli with various things. Thus the various stimuli become not simply stimuli to which a fixed response is automatically called forth, but they constitute for the animal a system of signals of the external world and of its own relations to the external world, to which a whole variety of responses are made.

Thus the animal becomes actively aware of things. To be

aware of things is essentially an active state, and not a passive state. To be aware of things is not simply to be affected by them, but to respond to them.

Awareness means first of all that the animal, by the use of its sense organs, discriminates certain features of its environment from the total environment, and responds to them. For example, it picks out its food by smell, touch and sight, and eats it.

And awareness means, secondly, that the animal attaches a meaning to various features of its environment, in the sense that it connects them with other things. For example, certain things become for the animal signals of the presence of food, or of the approach of something dangerous, and so on, and the animal responds accordingly.

Thus the active awareness of things which is engendered by the formation of conditioned reflexes means that the animal learns to connect the stimuli which it actually receives with other things by which it is not at the time directly affected. And so it is able to form expectations and to learn by experience.

In this way the formation of conditioned reflexes gives rise to the difference between the subjective and the objective. This difference, which has been the subject of much speculation and mystification by philosophers, has a natural explanation. For the difference between the subjective and the objective begins to arise as soon as animals begin to be aware of things. It is simply the difference between the totality of actually existing material conditions and the aspects of them of which the animal is aware and the meaning it attaches to them.

Hence the subjective as opposed to the objective, the mental as opposed to the physical, awareness as opposed to that which it is awareness of—all these differences arise as a result of the development of the higher nervous activity of animals through the building up by conditioned reflexes of ever more complicated relations of the animal with the external world.

The subjective is different from the objective, because (a) the animal is aware only of some parts or aspects and not of the whole of its surroundings, and (b) the meaning it attaches to things may be wrong—that is to say, things may become connected together subjectively in different ways from those in which they are connected together objectively, in actual fact.

And the objective is prior to the subjective, because (a) the existence of things is a condition for awareness of them whereas awareness of things is not a condition for their existence, and (b) things existed long before any awareness of them arose or could have arisen on the part of living organisms.

It is, then, in the activity of the nervous system—the activity of building complicated and variable relations with the external world—that *consciousness* arises. When, through the formation of conditioned reflexes, the stimulations which an animal receives begin to function for it as signals, and it learns to recognise such signals and to regulate its behaviour in accordance with them, then a new quality comes into existence in the nervous process of the animal, namely, consciousness.

Consciousness is not a mysterious " something " which comes into being parallel to, side by side with, the material life process of the brain. It is rather the new quality which distinguishes that life process. The brain process becomes a conscious process as a result of the brain's functioning as " the organ of the most complicated relations of the animal to the external world ". Consciousness is the peculiar quality of the relationship of the animal to the external world effected by the life process of the brain. This relationship becomes one in which the animal is aware of its surroundings through the stimulations of the various centres of its brain and the connections established in the brain. In so far as an animal lives in such relationship with its surroundings, it is conscious and its existence is conscious existence.

The elementary form of consciousness amongst animals is sensory consciousness, or sensation. This arises when, through the formation of conditioned reflexes, various stimulations of its sense organs acquire a meaning and become signals for the animal. For an external observer, these stimulations are simply modifications of the sense organs to which the animal responds in definite ways. But the life of the animal has then become a sensuously conscious life. Its brain process, or rather, a part of its brain process, has become a conscious process in which stimulations of the sense organs become sensations.

The difference between objective and subjective having arisen in the life of the animal, its sensations constitute the actual content of the subjective aspect of its life, in other words, the content of its consciousness. All its sensations are for it signals of definite things and connections with things.

Hence Pavlov said that sensations are the "subjective signals" of "the objective relations of the organism to the external world". And he said that in its sensations the animal possesses a "signal system", that is to say, a system of such subjective signals.

Acquiring such a signal system, the animal thereby acquires experience and the capacity to learn from experience. This is the great new thing in life which comes into being with sensory consciousness, and which has developed with the gradual evolution of the higher forms of animal life from the lower.

In the development of sensory consciousness in the higher animals, *sensation* passes into *perception*.

By the term "sensation" we denote the particular signals of connections between the animal and the external world resulting from the different stimulations of the different sense organs. Thus there are sensations of light or colour from the eyes, of sound from the ears, of smell from the nose, and so on. Many psychologists and philosophers have regarded sensation as simply a passive receiving of stimulations by the sense organs; for this reason, they often called sensations "impressions", implying that the sensation was simply a mark of the external object "impressed" on the sense organ. But on the contrary, sensation is essentially an activity of the brain, an active response in the sensory parts of the brain to the stimulations of the sense organs. A stimulus received by a sense organ only becomes a sensation when it passes into this activity of the brain, and becomes a signal of some connection with the external world.

Sensation develops into perception when in this sensory

activity of the brain there takes place the integration of the responses to many sense-stimulations. Continually responding to and recognising the signals received from its senses, the animal learns to relate sensations together so that together they afford a complex representation of complex objects in complex relations—and this is what we call "perception", as distinct from "sensation". By "perception" we denote the sensory awareness of complex objects in complex relations which, in the higher animals, is the product of their sensations. Perception is thus a development in use of the signal system of sensation.

Development of the Higher Mental Activity of Man

Pavlov went on to lay the foundations of the investigation of the higher mental activity of man—of speech and thought.

In their sensations all the higher animals, including man, possess a signal system, a system of signals of the objective relations of the animal and the external world; and from this they derive their perceptions. Pavlov went on to point out that, in addition to the signal system which man possesses in common with the animals, man also possesses another, a second signal system, which is specific only to the human being.

"When the developing animal world reached the stage of man," wrote Pavlov, "an extremely important addition was made to the mechanism of the higher nervous activity." With the animal, its surroundings and its own relationship with those surroundings are signalised by stimulations of the sense organs through the active response to those stimulations in the sensory parts of the brain. In other words, the animal becomes aware of its surroundings through sensations, and this awareness develops into perception. This is also true of men, since we are sensuously aware of the world around us through our sensations and perceptions. "This is the first system of signals, common to man and the animals," wrote Pavlov. "But *speech* constitutes a second system of signals of reality, which is peculiarly ours, and is a signal of the first signals."

Pavlov, then, regarded human speech as a "second signal

system ", developed through the activity of the human brain as an addition to the first signal system of sensations. And he regarded the development of this second signal system as the basis of development of all the higher mental activity of man.

Pavlov referred to sensations, the first signals of reality, which man possesses in common with the animals, as " concrete signals ". They are signals of concrete particular objects and of immediate connections with concrete particular objects.

Suppose, for example, that I am looking for something— for a collar stud dropped on the floor, let us say. Then a particular visual sensation is the signal for me that I have found what I am looking for. This particular sensation is the signal for me of the present whereabouts of a concrete particular object.

Words, on the other hand, function as signals in a different way. They function, said Pavlov, not as the first signals, sensations, do, as signals of concrete particular objects, but rather as " signals of the first signals".

Thus, for example, if I say to someone, " Please help me look for my collar stud ", the words " collar stud " function as the signal to him and to me of the kind of sensation associated with the thing we are looking for. And certainly, the other will not have understood me and the words will have failed in their signal function in his case, unless the words I use do thus function as " signals of the first signals "—that is to say, unless they are associated with definite sensations, with a definite kind of experience.

Because speech thus arises as a system of " signals of the first signals ", it follows that what we say depends on our own intention. What sensations we have depends on what external objects or internal bodily processes evoke the sensations. Our sensations depend on what is actually present, here and now. But there is no such limitation to the capacity of using words.

It therefore further follows that the speech signals, as Pavlov said, " represent an abstraction from reality and permit the forming of generalisations, which constitute our extra, specifically human, higher mentality ".

Because they function as " signals of the first signals " and not as " concrete signals ", words refer not merely to concrete particular objects which make their presence immediately felt in sensations but to the things in general which produce sensations of a definite kind. By words the speaker refers to the kinds of things and connections with things which are signalled by sensations, and not only to concrete particular things and connections. Hence words perform an abstracting, generalising function, because speech is capable of referring to objects in general and to general connections between objects. From this abstracting, generalising function of the second signal system, of speech, proceeds the entire higher mental life peculiar to man, the formation of concepts and the exercise of thought.

The second signal system, speech, arises and functions only in inseparable connection with the first, from which it evolved and from which it cannot in any circumstances be separated. The two signal systems in the human brain are in continual interaction. Therefore it can never be correct to consider the development of the second as something separate from the first—to consider the thought of man as developing independently of his sensation, to consider human thought as developing independently of the concrete conditions of men's material life. Without sensation, there can be no speech and no thought, since the second signals develop only as signals of the first signals. At the same time, the development of the first signal system in man is also conditioned by that of the second. The development of man's perceptions of things is conditioned and directed by his ideas about them. This is shown, for example, by the fact that in children the naming of things is an indispensable part of the education of their senses.

To understand the connection of the second signal system with the first, and the function of abstraction and generalisation performed by the second signal system, we must remember that in building up conditioned connections with things through sensations the animal is already learning to react to and so distinguish what is common to different things—that is to say, it is already recognising the universal or general in the particular.

For example, a dog associates different smells with different things ; and this means that it recognises the same smell when it occurs on different occasions. In other words, it recognises the general in the particular. Clearly, a smell on one lamp-post and a smell on another lamp-post are two smells ; but the dog is able to recognise them as the same smell, and its nose picks out what is common between them. What is common to the two similar sensations received from sniffing at two lamp-posts is a signal to the dog that another dog has visited each lamp-post.

When men use words as a second signal system, the different words are used to pick out, to abstract and generalise, what is common between different sensations. All words perform this function of abstracting the general from the particular. Man does not merely recognise the general in the particular as animals do, but abstracts it from the particular by finding a word for it.

First there must be sensations and the recognition of the universal in the particular through sensations. Only after that can follow the abstraction of the universal from the particular by means of words.

The development in man of the second signal system from the first is socially determined. It is explained by the fact that men relate themselves to their surroundings not only in the ways other animals do but, in human society, in different and specifically new ways. Something qualitatively new appears in human behaviour and, therefore, something new in the functioning of the human brain. In using their hands to make instruments of production men have created human society and entirely transformed their way of life from animal to human life. It is in this process—in social life and in response to the requirements of social life—that speech is developed. The second signal system of speech is developed by the human brain as a result of the productive activity and social intercourse of men.

CHAPTER TWO

MIND AS PRODUCT AND REFLECTION OF MATTER

The essential feature of mental processes is that in and through them the organism continually builds up complicated and variable relations with its surroundings. The processes of consciousness, therefore, are processes reflecting external, material reality. Consciousness consists in the reflection of the material world in the life process of the brain.

Mental Processes are Processes of the Brain, Relating the Organism to its Surroundings.

PAVLOV'S investigations confirm, amplify and develop the views about the relations of matter and mind taken by the founders of Marxism. We shall in this chapter briefly summarise the fundamentals of these views, contrasting them with the views held by idealism.

(1) Idealism holds that mental functions are functions of a mind which can exist in separation from the body.

But Marxism holds that mental functions are functions of highly developed matter, namely, of the brain. Mental processes are brain processes, processes of a material, bodily organ.

The essential feature of mental processes is that in and through them the animal continually builds up most complicated and variable relations with its surroundings. When we perceive things we are relating ourselves to external objects through the perceptual activity of the brain. And when we think of things, we are relating ourselves to external objects through the thought activity of the brain.

Considering that consciousness belongs to a mind which exists in separation from matter, idealism relies upon the method of introspection in order to give an account of our consciousness. This is the method of looking inside one's own consciousness, so to speak, and trying to analyse what is found there.

The outstanding example of the use of the introspective method in modern psychology is psycho-analysis. Psycho-analysis has evolved a special technique of controlled introspection, applied by the co-operation of a patient and a psycho-analyst. By inducing the patient to report on whatever comes into his mind, to relate his dreams, and so on, the psycho-analyst claims to discover beneath consciousness a whole realm of the unconscious. And so there has been developed a very elaborate theory of the different parts of the mind and of their relations and functions—of the conscious and the unconscious, the ego, the id and the super-ego. This is but an extension of the method used by all idealist philosophers and psychologists when they try to analyse the constituent parts of the human mind, classifying them, relating them and trying to trace their development, all the time treating consciousness as though it were a world on its own, divorced from the external material world.

Adopting such a method, many idealist philosophers have come to the conclusion that the perceptions and ideas which constitute the content of consciousness are a special kind of objects which have a mental existence distinct from the material existence of objects outside our consciousness.

For such idealist philosophers, what we are aware of in our conscious life is not material objects at all. We know only our ideas of things, and not the "things in themselves". Thus the English philosopher John Locke wrote: "The mind, in all its thoughts and reasonings, hath no other immediate object but its own ideas, which it alone does or can contemplate."[1]

Hence idealists conclude that only God knows what are the properties of "things in themselves", for they consider our sensations and ideas to be a kind of wall inside our consciousness, cutting it off from the external world. Some go a step further, and conclude that there is no reason to believe that external,

[1] Locke, *Essay on the Human Understanding*, I, I, 8.

material things exist at all : nothing exists except our minds and the sensations and ideas in our minds. " If there were external bodies ", wrote George Berkeley, " it is impossible we should ever come to know it ; and if there were not, we might have the very same reasons to think there were as we have now."[1]

But there is another method of studying our consciousness, namely, the method of science, which studies living, conscious organisms in their active relationship with their surroundings. This is the method which was adopted by Marx and Engels and, independently, by Pavlov. This method does not treat consciousness as a special object of introspective contemplation. On the contrary, it considers that, as Marx and Engels expressed it, " consciousness is always conscious existence ".[2] And so it does not study consciousness as though it were something existing in abstraction from the life process of living, conscious organisms, but, on the contrary, it studies their conscious activity.

As we have said, the essence of conscious activity is to build up complicated and variable active relations between the conscious organism and its surroundings, and this function is performed by the brain. Consequently the processes of consciousness are processes whereby we relate ourselves to the external world. Far from standing in the way of our apprehension of external things, our sensations and ideas are the means whereby we apprehend them.

" Sensation is the direct connection between consciousness and the external world", wrote Lenin. " The sophism of idealist philosophy consists in the fact that it regards sensation as being not the connection between consciousness and the external world, but as a fence, a wall, separating consciousness from the external world."[3]

Adopting the scientific approach to the nature of consciousness, Marxism therefore denies the idealist theory that when we perceive, feel or think there are *two separate processes* going

[1] Berkeley, *Principles of Human Knowledge*, 20.
[2] Marx and Engels, *The German Ideology*, Part I.
[3] Lenin, *Materialism and Empirio-Criticism*, ch. 1, section 1.

on—the material process of the brain and the mental process of consciousness. Marxism considers that *only one* process is involved, namely, the material process of the brain. Mental processes are simply one aspect of the processes of the functioning of the brain as the organ of most complicated relations to the external world.

And so Marx wrote that thinking is " the life process of the human brain".[1]

Consciousness is a Product of the Development of Matter

(2) According to idealism, such phenomena as perceptions, feelings and thoughts could not be produced by the workings of any material system. Idealism holds that the peculiar quality of consciousness which distinguishes mental processes cannot be explained as arising from any possible combination of material conditions, but is a quality absolutely incompatible with all qualities of material systems. Such a quality, idealism concludes, can belong only to something non-material, namely, the mind.

But Marxism holds that consciousness is a product of the development of matter, namely, of living bodies with a central nervous system, and that perceptions, feelings and thoughts are, in fact, the highest products of matter.

" If the question is raised : what, then, are thought and consciousness and whence they came," wrote Engels, " it becomes apparent that they are products of the human brain, and that man himself is a product of nature, which has been developed in and along with his environment."[2]

" The material, sensuously perceptible world to which we belong is the only reality," Engels further wrote. " Our consciousness and thinking, however suprasensuous they may seem, are the products of a material, bodily organ, the brain. Matter is not a product of mind, but mind itself is merely the highest product of nature."[3]

[1] Marx, *Capital*, Preface to 2nd edition.
[2] Engels, *Anti-Duhring*, Part I, ch. 3.
[3] Engels, *Ludwig Feuerbach*, ch. 2.

When animals develop a nervous system and begin actively to relate themselves to their environment by conditioned connections, then the nervous process becomes a conscious process, a process of sensation and, in man, of thinking. Hence sensations and thoughts are the peculiar products of the nervous process.

Sensation, wrote Lenin, is " one of the properties of matter in motion".[1]

" Matter acting on our sense-organs produces sensation," he continued. " Sensation depends on the brain, nerves, retina, etc., i.e., on matter organised in a definite way. . . . Sensation, thought, consciousness are the supreme product of matter organised in a particular way."[2]

Consciousness is Reflection of the Material World

(3) Idealism, which holds that the mind exists in separation from the body and that perceptions and thoughts cannot be products of any material process, holds that perceptions and thoughts are creations of the mind which occupy our consciousness independently of the existence of external, material things.

But Marxism holds that perceptions and thoughts are nothing but reflections of material things. The processes of consciousness are processes reflecting external, material reality, and nothing can come to birth in consciousness except as a reflection of the material world.

Marx wrote that " the ideal is nothing else than the material world reflected by the human mind and translated into forms of thought".[3]

He considered that in the process of thinking, and in consciousness in general, there is produced a reflection of different parts or aspects of the material world in one particular material process, namely, the life process of the brain. In our consciousness, different parts or aspects of the material world are translated into forms of consciousness—perceptions and

[1] Lenin, *loc. cit.*
[2] Lenin, *loc. cit.*, section 2.
[3] Marx, *loc. cit.*

thoughts. They are reproduced in the life activity of the brain, in forms appropriate to that activity.

Thus, for example, the properties of various bodies absorbing and reflecting light are, in the sensory activity of the brain, reproduced in the form of sensations of colour. Again, the relations and common features of things are, in the thinking activity of the brain, reproduced in the form of concepts.

What exactly do we mean by " reflection ", when we say that consciousness is a reflection of material reality ? There are four features of the process of reflection to which we may specially draw attention.

Material Reality is Primary and its Mental Reflection is Secondary or Derivative

(a) The process of reflection involves a relationship between two separate material processes, such that features of the first process are reproduced in corresponding features of the second process. The first process is primary, and its reflection in the second is secondary or derivative. For the first process develops in complete independence of the second, whereas the reproduction of features of the first process by reflection in the second could not occur unless those features were first there to be reproduced or reflected.

This fundamental feature of any process of reflection is illustrated by reflection in a mirror—although, as we shall see, the active reflection of external reality in consciousness differs in important respects from the passive reflection which takes place in a mirror.

Thus when objects are reflected in a mirror, those objects which are set before the mirror do not depend on being reflected in the mirror for either their existence or their characteristics ; but, on the other hand, the reflection in the mirror depends on what is set before the mirror, and nothing is reflected in the mirror which does not reproduce in some way the characteristics of what is set before the mirror. Hence the object is primary, and its reflection secondary or derivative.

Similarly, the existence of material objects does not depend on our being conscious of them ; but, on the other hand, there is nothing in our consciousness which does not reproduce in some way or other something which exists in the material world.

There are many characteristics of things which are not reproduced in our sensations ; but we have no sensation which does not correspond, in some way or other, to some definite characteristic of things. There are many relations of things and common features of things which are not reproduced in our concepts ; but we can form no concept in our minds which does not reproduce, in some way or other, even if in fantastic ways (as in a distorting mirror), some features or some relationship of things.

Of course, many concepts give an appearance of having no basis in the reflection of material reality, just because, once formed, concepts can be freely combined in all sorts of fantastic ways. For example, everyone knows that no real animal is reflected in the concept of a mermaid, but that this concept is formed by combining ideas of real animals, namely, of women and fishes. Similarly, materialists can consistently argue that no real object corresponds to the concept of God as a trinity of persons with infinite power and infinite knowledge, but that the several concepts of persons, power, knowledge and infinity have all been formed as reflections of material reality.

When we say, therefore, that material reality is reflected in consciousness, we mean that features of material reality are reproduced in consciousness, and that material reality is primary and its reproduction in consciousness secondary or derivative.

" Our consciousness is only an image of the external world," wrote Lenin, " and it is obvious that an image cannot exist without the thing imaged, and that the latter exists independently of that which images it."[1]

" Matter is primary," wrote Stalin, " since it is the source of sensations, ideas, mind ; and mind is secondary, derivative, since it is a reflection of matter."[2]

[1] Lenin, *loc. cit.*, section 3.
[2] Stalin, *Dialectical and Historical Materialism.*

Material Reality is Reflected in Consciousness in Forms Determined
by the Activity of the Brain

(b) What exists in one form in the primary process is reproduced in another form in the secondary process of reflection. What exists independently in one form is, so to speak, translated into another form in the process of reflection. The process of reflection is therefore a process of translation or transformation from one form into another. And the form of the reflection depends, of course, on the nature of the process of reflection.

When we say, therefore, that material reality is reflected in consciousness, we mean that features of material processes are reproduced—in another material process, namely, in the life process of the brain—in special forms, namely, in the forms of perceptions and thoughts.

These forms are created in the operation of the processes of the brain, namely, in the operation of the first and second signal systems of the brain.

Material reality is thus reproduced or reflected in consciousness in forms created by and adapted to the practical requirements of living, conscious organisms.

Our sensations, for example, are the reflections in the conscious process of our brains of features of material things. Those features are not, however, themselves sensations but are reflected in sensations, and our sensations are the form in which we are perceptually conscious of them and so are able to react to them.

Thus when we see colours, for instance, we are not seeing things which exist only in our minds—as some philosophers have asserted—but are seeing things which exist independently, outside our minds, the properties of which are reflected in our sensations of colour. Properties which exist in real things as properties of the absorption and reflection of light are reflected in our perceptual consciousness in the form of sensations of colour.

Thus Lenin wrote : " If colour is a sensation only depending on the retina (as natural science compels you to admit), then light rays, falling upon the retina, produce the sensation of colour. This means that outside us, independently of us and of our minds, there exists a movement of matter . . . which, acting upon the retina, produces in man the sensation of a particular colour. This is precisely how natural science regards it. It explains the sensations of various colours by the various lengths of light-waves existing outside the human retina, outside man and independently of him."[1]

Thought, again, produces a more abstract, more general reflection of reality than perception. In what form is reality reflected in our thoughts ? It is reflected in the form of propositions. Thought issues in propositions in which, for example, a subject is combined with a predicate. The material world does not exist in the form of a combination of subjects and predicates. This combination is a product of the second signal system, of the thinking activity of the brain, and through it reality is reflected in thought. This is how the material world is " translated into forms of thought".

Consider, for example, any object—a red pencil, say. When we think about such an object we express our conclusions about it in propositions, such as, " This pencil is red ". This proposition is divided into a subject and predicate, which are combined in the proposition. But the object is not so divided in concrete reality. A red pencil does not divide into two parts— a subject, the pencil, and a predicate, red. Nevertheless, it is obvious that when we say, " This pencil is red ", the proposition does reflect the objective reality of the pencil, which is thus correctly " translated into forms of thought ".

The Reflection of Material Reality in Consciousness Takes Place through the Active Relationship of the Living Organism and its Surroundings

(c) Reflection is always a product of the relationship and inter-action of the process in which the reflection occurs and the primary process which is reflected. Its source is the primary process.

[1] Lenin, *loc. cit.*, section 2.

Thus the life process of the brain reproduces or reflects in its products—perceptions and thoughts—the surrounding material reality, which is the source of all perceptions and thoughts. And this reflection takes place in, and is the result of, the interaction of the conscious organism with its environment. This interaction is regulated by the brain, as the organ of the most complicated relations of the animal to its environment. The brain is continually active in the process of reflection, continually producing the reflection of external objects in consciousness.

It follows, therefore, that the way in which the material world is reflected in consciousness is governed by the active relationship between the living conscious organism and its surroundings, by the circumstances of the animal, by its internal state as well as by its external relations.

When we take this into account, it becomes obvious that in the process of reflection of external reality in our consciousness, the objects reflected can become considerably altered in the reflection. For the reflection is not at all like a direct mirror-image of the object, but is the product of a complex process of interaction in which the brain is continually active.

This accounts for the well known fact that our perceptions of objects are very often misleading; they may misrepresent objects, or even (as in certain illusions and hallucinations) lead us to suppose that objects are present which are not really there at all.

Many philosophers have opposed the materialist view that consciousness reflects external reality. And one of the arguments they have advanced for opposing this view is based simply on the character of our perceptions.

"Take a penny," they say. "You believe that the material penny has a definite shape and size, and that this material object is reflected in your perceptions when you look at it. Very well. If you look at this penny from a distance it looks small, while if you hold it close to your eye it looks big; if you hold it one way it looks circular, while if you hold it another way it looks elliptical. In fact, your perceptions of it change in all sorts of ways, while the material object, of which your perceptions are alleged to be the images in your mind, does not change at all. How, then, can perceptions be said to reflect external reality, since they change while the latter does not ? "

This question, which is so confidently posed as an unanswerable argument against the theory of reflection, can be very easily answered. The philosophers who argue in such a way have simply forgotten that reflection is an active process, conditioned by the actual relations between the organism and its surroundings.

Thus if we look at the same thing from different distances or from different angles, then of course it will be differently reflected in our perceptions—its size or shape will differ. Again, if we see a thing through different mediums, of course it will look different—as when a straight stick held in the water looks bent. Again, the reflection will necessarily be altered by the actual state of our sense organs—press the corner of your eye, and you will see two of everything ; make one hand hot and the other cold, and plunge them both into a bowl of water, and the water will feel colder to one hand than to the other. Lastly, since perceiving is an activity of the brain, it is not surprising that, objects having been once reflected in that activity, the brain can reproduce reflections of those objects under certain circumstances even when they are not there—as in dreams, illusions of all kinds and hallucinations.

Still more in the processes of thought can we misrepresent to ourselves the properties of things, ascribe to them properties which they do not possess, and think of things which do not exist at all. By means of thought we often correct illusions occurring in perception. But we also often produce new and greater illusions.

The Reflection of Reality in Consciousness is an Active Factor in Directing the Practice of Changing Reality

(d) The fact that reflection in consciousness is the product of life activity, of the activity of the organism in relation to its surroundings, means that the consciousness of man, both his perceptions and his thoughts, is continually conditioned by his experience and his social activity. What men perceive and what they think does not arise by a direct process of the reproduction of external reality in perception and thought, but is conditioned by their experience, manner of life and social relations.

Thus it is well known that differences in people's experience and manner of life determine differences in what they perceive in things. The perceptions of a skilled engineer examining a complex machine, for example, are not the same as those of a man not familiar with such machines, although their sense organs may be affected in precisely similar ways. The perceptions of a farmer looking at a country scene are not the same as those of a townsman, and an artist perceives the same scene in still other ways.

Still greater are the differences which arise between men's concepts and thoughts about things on the basis of differences in class, experience and upbringing.

In the human being, moreover, ideas about things also exert an influence back on perceptions. The fact that we do not merely perceive things but form ideas of them influences perception—in other words, the operations of the second signal system in man, which in the first place arise out of the operations of the first signal system, react back upon the first. This was exemplified, indeed, in the examples just cited. If a skilled engineer perceives more in a machine than other men do, this is because he has more ideas about it than they. Again, while artists may perceive more in things than inartistic people, different artists also perceive things differently according to their ideas of them. This is shown, for example, in the very different ways in which painters of different outlook portray human beings ; some portray the strength and nobility of men, while others perceive nothing of the kind in the subjects of their paintings.

The reflection of our surroundings and of our connections with our surroundings in our consciousness is a very active factor in determining our activity of changing our surroundings. The fact that consciousness is reflection does not mean that consciousness is not an active factor in life. Consciousness is in the first place a product of life activity, in the second place it is a product which plays a major part in directing that very activity of which it is a product. In consciousness, life has produced the means of directing life towards definite ends.

Indeed, we can say that that is why consciousness was bound to be produced in the course of the evolution of living organisms.

Conscious existence is life activity governed by the reflection of external conditions in the brain. This reflection is, in the first place, a product of the active relationships of the conscious organism to its surroundings; and, in turn, it actively conditions the further development of those relationships through the practice of men in changing their surroundings. Man's consciousness is a product of his practice which plays the part of directing his practice.

Finally, in considering this active role of consciousness we should bear in mind that the reflection of the material world in consciousness does not take the form only of perceptions and thoughts. In his active, conscious existence man also feels emotions.

According to many idealists, emotions well up out of man's inner spiritual being. But for materialism, emotions, too, are modes of the reflection of material reality in the consciousness of man. They reflect the active relationship of man to his environment. And being active, being affected by things in his activity, and taking a definite attitude towards things and possible changes in things, man feels emotions about things and is impelled in his activity by emotions. In his conscious existence man is not only aware of things in perception and thought, but also feels his active relationship to things emotionally.

Emotional consciousness is, then, a necessary part of life. A man relates himself to surrounding reality by perceiving it and forming ideas about it, but this relationship needs to be completed by the emotions he feels about it. Similarly, emotions need to be guided and directed by perceptions and ideas.

Matter and its Reflection

To conclude.

There is no consciousness apart from a living brain. The source of all consciousness, of everything that enters into consciousness, is the material world. In consciousness there occurs the reflection of the material world in the life process of the brain, and this reflection is what constitutes the content of consciousness.

There are not, therefore, two separate and distinct spheres of existence, material and spiritual. There are not two worlds, the material and the spiritual worlds. But there exists only the material world, only material processes.

In the course of material development there arises the reflection of material processes in one particular material process, the life process of the brain. And when we distinguish material and spiritual, matter and mind, what we are distinguishing is simply material being, movement in space and time, from its reflection in the life process of the brain.

The process which gives rise to the reflection and the process in which the reflection occurs are both material processes. But the reflection is not material but mental—that is to say, not material but a reflection of matter.

" The materialist elimination of the ' dualism of spirit and body '," wrote Lenin, " consists in the assertion that spirit does not exist independently of the body, that spirit is secondary, a function of the brain, a reflection of the external world."[1]

" The antithesis of matter and mind has absolute significance only within the bounds of a very limited field," he concluded, " exclusively within the bounds of the fundamental problem of what is to be regarded as primary and what as secondary. Beyond these bounds the relative character of this antithesis is indubitable."[2]

[1] Lenin, *loc. cit.*, section 5.
[2] Lenin, *loc. cit.*, ch. 3, section 1.

CHAPTER THREE

SOCIAL LABOUR AND SOCIAL THINKING

The development of man's mental functions arises from his social activity, proceeding from perception to thought. The capacity to think and to speak originates from the process of social labour, which is man's fundamental social activity.

The Human Brain and What We Do with It

THE human brain, which alone is capable of producing general ideas, conceptual consciousness, thinking, is the product of a long evolution of the forms of life. It is the culmination of a process of evolution in the size and structure of the brain. In particular, the cerebral cortex is far larger in man than in other animals, and a large part of the cortex has come to be specially concerned with controlling the hands and the organs of speech.

It is true that we are only at the beginning of scientific knowledge of how the brain works. But enough is known to assert confidently that the brain is the organ of thought, that thinking is done by the brain, and that the evolution of a certain size and structure of the brain was necessary as a condition of our being able to think with it.

The biological evolution of the brain into an organ capable of thinking took place in the pre-human stage of the evolution of man, in that stage during which ape-like animals were evolving into men. The decisive step in man's evolution was probably taken when an erect posture was adopted by these animals. For this set free the hand, with which the whole of man's productive activity has been accomplished. With the use of the hand went the physical development of the hand into the human hand, and with that, the development of the brain which controls the hand into the human brain.

The first men already had the same kinds of brains as we have, just as they had the same kinds of hands, feet, eyes, noses, teeth, stomachs and so on. Our organs, including our brains, are no different from theirs, although in the meantime we have learned to do many things which they did not do.

Thus once biological evolution had produced the human brain and hands, man started a new kind of evolution of his own. The evolution of man is not biological. What man evolves is his social organisation, his techniques, his culture and his knowledge, his conscious mastery over himself and external nature.

Hence in relation to the brain, what has developed since man first came into existence is not his brain but the use he has made of it—his development of the capacities contained in it. Man has developed his material activities, his perceptions and his thoughts ; and through doing this has continually revolutionised his own conditions of life and increased his capacities and powers.

From Perceptions to Ideas

Thinking arises only out of sense-perception and must be preceded by it. To think about the world we must first perceive the world. We can form no concept that is not based on and prompted by perception. And in general, no ideas at all are formed without the perceptions which are the necessary material on which the activity of thinking has to work.

A man isolated from childhood in a confined space, for instance, might have as good a brain as anyone else, but he would have very little to think about, and his ideas and the range of his ideas would be very limited. Similarly, the range of ideas of primitive peoples is limited as compared with civilised men, though their brains are in no way inferior.

It is as our perceptions increase with increased activity and social contacts that our ideas develop.

Thinking, then, grows out of perception. And this development takes place only in and through the active relationship to the external world which men establish for themselves in the course of their practical social activity. Perception itself is not just a passive receiving of impressions from external objects. The development of sensation into perception is the product of the development of active relationships to the external world. And the more varied and complex is the active relationship of the organism to its surroundings, the more varied and complex will be the content of the perception of those surroundings.

" The real intellectual wealth of the individual depends entirely on the wealth of his real connections," wrote Marx and Engels.[1]

Human perception is much wider in scope than that of any other animal. And this is because man has wider activities and interests, and in developing these activities and interests has effected a corresponding development of his senses. It is because man has developed his activities and his perceptions that he has been able to think and to develop his ideas—and this has then reacted back again on the further development of his activities and of his perceptions.

" The eagle sees much further than man, but the human eye sees considerably more in things than does the eye of the eagle," wrote Engels. " The dog has a far keener sense of smell than man, but it does not distinguish a hundredth part of the odours that for man are definite features of different things. And the sense of touch, which the ape hardly possesses in its crudest initial form, has been developed side by side with the development of the human hand itself, through the medium of labour."[2]

The basis for this heightened perception and wider range of perception in man was established by our early ancestors, when they first began to stand erect, to look around them, and to use their hands, not to swing among the branches of trees and grab food, but to fashion tools and implements.

As man's activity developed, so there developed the wealth

[1] Marx and Engels, *The German Ideology*, Part 1, section 2.
[2] Engels, *Dialectics of Nature*, ch. 9: *The Part Played by Labour in the Transition from Ape to Man.*

of his connections with the world around him. Man achieved a heightened perception and wider scope of perceptions, and then the second signal system of speech, which marks the transition from concrete sense-perceptions to abstract, general ideas. The interaction in the course of man's activity of the second signal system with the first led to the still greater development of his perceptions, and so again to the further development of ideas.

The capacity of the human brain to perceive and then to think is realised and developed in human activity.

Labour

Man lives in society, and acts together with his fellow men. His whole mode of life is social. Therefore just as it is in his social activity that he enlarges his perceptions, so it is in his social activity that, starting from these perceptions, he begins to form ideas, to think and to develop his ideas.

The basis of man's social activity is labour. It is in and through labour that man first of all enlarges his perceptions and first of all begins to use his brain to think—to form ideas and to communicate them, to develop thought and language.

In labour, then, is to be found the source and origin of thought and language.

" Labour . . . is the primary basic condition of all human existence," wrote Engels, " and this to such an extent that, in a sense, we have to say that labour created man himself."[1]

In the evolution of man, Engels pointed out,[2] the first decisive step was taken when an erect posture was adopted. This set free the hand. And when men began to fashion tools and implements with their hands for use in changing external objects and producing the means of life, that was the real beginning of men and of human society.

" The first premise of all human history is, of course, the existence of living human individuals," wrote Marx and Engels. " Thus the first fact to be established is the physical organisation of these individuals and their consequent relation to the rest

[1] *Ibid.*   [2] *Ibid.*

of nature." But having established that fact, it is necessary to establish what they do—their activity, their mode of life. " Men . . . begin to distinguish themselves from animals as soon as they begin to produce their means of subsistence, a step which is conditioned by their physical organisation. By producing their means of subsistence men are indirectly producing their actual material life."[1]

It is in producing their means of subsistence and so indirectly producing their actual material life that men, conditioned by their physical organisation, begin to act as men, to develop social organisation and " make their own history," and in so doing to form ideas, to think and to speak.

Distinctive Features of Human Labour

What are the distinctive features of human labour, as compared with the ways in which other animals secure the means of life ?

(1) First, men fashion tools and implements, changing natural objects so as to use their properties to bring about desired ends.

" An instrument of labour", wrote Marx, " is a thing, or a complex of things, which the labourer interposes between himself and the subject of his labour, and which serves as the conductor of his activity. He makes use of the mechanical, physical and chemical properties of some substances in order to make other substances subservient to his aims."[2]

The animal, on the other hand, collects and rearranges objects to hand, but does not transform them and use their properties and the natural forces contained in them for producing his means of life and affecting large-scale transformation of his surroundings in accordance with his own needs.

" The tool implies specific human activity, the transforming reaction of man on nature, production," wrote Engels. "Animals in the narrower sense also have tools, but only as limbs of their bodies : the ant, the bee, the beaver. Animals also produce,

[1] Marx and Engels, *The German Ideology*, Part I, ch. 1.
[2] Marx, *Capital*, Vol. I, ch. 7, section 1.

but their productive effort on surrounding nature in relation to the latter amounts to nothing at all. Man alone has succeeded in impressing his stamp on nature, not only by shifting the plant and animal world from one place to another, but also by so altering the aspect and climate of his dwelling place, and even the plants and animals themselves, that the consequences of his activity can disappear only with the general extinction of the terrestrial globe."[1]

" Animals change external nature by their activities just as man does, if not to the same extent," Engels further wrote. " . . . But if animals exert a lasting effect on their environment, it happens unintentionally, and, as far as the animals are concerned, it is an accident. The further men become removed from the animals, however, the more their effect on nature assumes the character of a premeditated, planned action, directed towards definite ends known in advance . . .

" In short the animal merely *uses* external nature, and brings about changes in it simply by his presence ; man by his changes makes it serve his ends, *masters* it."[2]

By his labour, then, man masters nature, fashioning tools and using them so as to make nature serve his ends. " In the labour process," wrote Marx, " man's activity, with the help of the instruments of labour, effects an alteration, designed from the commencement, in the material worked upon."[3] And it is in thus mastering and changing nature that man changes himself, develops his own human attributes.

(2) The second distinctive feature of human labour follows from the first, and lies in its conscious and co-operative character.

In making tools and using them, in compelling natural objects and natural forces to serve his ends, man is conscious of his ends, has an idea of the result he intends to bring about. And men work co-operatively, according to a conscious design and plan, to bring about the ends they intend to achieve.

[1] Engels, *Dialectics of Nature*, Introduction.
[2] Engels, *Dialectics of Nature*, ch. 9 : *The Part Played by Labour in the Transition from Ape to Man.*
[3] Marx, *Capital*, Vol. I, ch. 7, section 1.

While such social creatures as bees, for example, build elaborate structures, they do so in an automatic way, by instinct. Human builders, on the other hand, work according to a conscious plan.

"We presuppose labour in a form which stamps it as exclusively human," wrote Marx. "A spider conducts operations that resemble those of a weaver, and a bee puts to shame many an architect in the construction of her cells. But what distinguishes the worst of architects from the best of bees is this, that the architect raises his structure in imagination before he erects it in reality. At the end of every labour process we get a result that already existed in the imagination of the labourer at its commencement."[1]

Labour, Speech and Thought

These distinctive features of labour—that labour is the use of tools and implements to effect changes of external objects by human beings co-operating to realise results which they consciously set before themselves—explain why labour necessarily gives rise to speech and thought, and cannot develop without the aids of speech and thought.

"The mastery over nature, which begins with the development of the hand, with labour, widened man's horizon at every new advance. He was continually discovering new, hitherto unknown properties of natural objects."[2]

In these words Engels points out that labour, even of the most primitive kind, as in the fashioning and use of hunting and fishing implements, makes men perceive things with a new interest, enlarges their perceptions, "widens their horizon", makes them aware through their practical activity and from their perceptions of ever more properties of natural objects. And indeed, from these first beginnings, it has always been through their advancing mastery over nature that succeeding generations of men have come to know more and more of the properties of natural objects: each stage of advance has

[1] Marx, *Capital*, Vol. I, ch. 7, section 1.
[2] Engels, *loc. cit.*

meant enlarged perceptions, new discoveries, wider horizons.

" On the other hand," Engels continues, " the development of labour necessarily helped to bring the members of society closer together by multiplying cases of mutual support and joint activity, and by making clear the advantage of this joint activity to each individual. In short, men in the making arrived at the point where *they had something to say* to one another."

This something which they " had to say to one another " concerned, in the first place, the properties of those objects which can be used by man, and the ends to be achieved and the results to be aimed at by human co-operation. And this is precisely something which can *only* be " said ", which can only be signalled and expressed by *articulate speech*, and not by calls and gestures such as are employed by the animals.

" The little that even the most highly developed animals need to communicate to one another can be communicated even without the aid of articulate speech," Engels pointed out.

Animals signal to one another the presence of particular objects—as in the gestures made by bees, the so-called dances by which they indicate the presence of a source of honey in a particular direction ; they arouse one another to particular actions—as in the call of the leader of a pack. But that is all. If their mode of life were such that they needed to communicate with one another about the different properties of things, about how these were to be used, and about the ends they aimed to achieve by different forms of co-operative activity, then such gestures and calls would no longer avail them. For they would then need to communicate not the particular but the general. Animals have no such need. But men do have such a need immediately they embark upon even the most elementary forms of social labour. They then have something they need to *say* to one another, as Engels pointed out. And so they develop the means to say it.

" The need led to the creation of its organ," Engels continues. " The undeveloped larynx of the ape was slowly but surely transformed by means of gradually increased modulation, and the organs of the mouth gradually learned to pronounce one articulate letter after another. Comparison with animals proves that this explanation of the origin of language from and in the process of labour is the only correct one."

Men needed to communicate with one another about the properties of objects and the practical use to be made of those properties. And Engels here describes how they developed the use of the larynx and the mouth in order to articulate words and sentences by which to effect this communication. This process has its counterpart in the individual brain—namely, the development, which Pavlov first described, of a second signal system, the speech signals. These signals are no longer, like sensations, signals only of immediate connections with external objects, but " represent an abstraction from reality and so permit the forming of generalisations".

Ideas

The second signal system marks the advance from the animal to the human brain, from sensation and perception to ideas.

Ideas do not merely reproduce objects immediately confronting us, representing them as they immediately appear to the individual through his senses. In ideas the properties and relations of objects are reproduced in abstraction. The idea of an object is not the image of a particular, sensuous thing but the idea of a kind of thing.

Consequently while we *perceive* only what is actually confronting us, according to the impression it makes on our sense organs, we can *think* of the objects which we perceive not merely in their given relations, with their given properties, but in different relations and with changed properties. For we form ideas of the different kinds of things and of their properties and relations in abstraction, and so can think out what we can do with the different kinds of things, or how we can change their properties for various purposes.

In this resides the power of thought. We can think of what is to be done with things, of changes which we intend to bring about, and can work out the means to achieve those changes. In thinking we work out experiments in our heads, as it were—representing what must be done, what must happen, in order that some changed state of affairs shall be realised. The conclusions of the experiment in thought are then checked by the results of practice. This is the very essence of the process of thinking, as it arises out of the process of labour.

We should here note that ideas are not the same as images. Thus the idea or concept of, for example, a colour or shape is not the same as the image of a colour or of a shape which we can form in the imagination. The older empiricist philosophers (especially Berkeley and Hume) used to confound ideas and images ; but, on the contrary, they should be carefully distinguished. Images are only a continuation of sensation, of the first signal system ; but ideas mark the development of a second signal system, representing an abstraction from reality and permitting the forming of generalisations.

No doubt the higher animals as well as man can form in their minds sensuous images of objects. For instance, a fox can no doubt picture to itself the process of finding, hunting, killing and eating a rabbit, and then proceed to turn this image into reality. It can, and does, show considerable cunning and foresight in carrying out its purpose. But a man who uses even the simplest instrument of production employs methods which no other animal could employ. To make and use even the simplest instruments of production, he must not only have pictured things to himself but have formed ideas of the properties of things which can be put to use in realising the ends he desired.

Thus we can see in what way thought is a higher form of consciousness than sense-perception. Sense-perception reproduces things as they immediately appear through their action on our sense organs. When we form ideas, on the other hand, we can think of things in their essential character apart from their particular existence and mode of appearance ; and so we can represent to ourselves in thought what transformations things undergo in different circumstances, how they interact, their various potentialities, interconnections and laws of change and motion.

It is evident, therefore, what a tremendous leap was made in the development of consciousness when ideas were formed. This leap to human consciousness was simply the ideal side of the leap from the animal to the human mode of life, made when men began to design and use tools.

Just as man no longer, like the animals, merely collects and rearranges and uses natural objects, but masters nature, so in his ideas he does not merely register the appearances of things, as in perception, but traces their interconnections and causes.

CHAPTER FOUR

THOUGHT, LANGUAGE AND LOGIC

The development of ideas is inseparable from the development of speech and language, and there can be no thought without language. The words and grammatical rules of language must always satisfy the common requirements of what is to be expressed in language, which are objective requirements independent of the particular conventions of particular languages. And these same requirements give rise to the laws of logic, or laws of thought, which are universal and necessary laws of the reflection of objective reality in thought.

Ideas and Language

THE power belonging to ideas, of representing things not merely in their immediate existence as presented to the senses but of representing properties and relations in abstraction from particular things—this power is a product of the second signal system in the human brain. The development of thinking and the power of thought are, therefore, inseparable from and dependent on the development and power of speech.

As we have said, sensations are signals of immediate connections with concrete particular objects. Words are " signals of the first signals ", and their reference is not only to particular, concrete things which are signalled by sensations but to the things in general which produce sensations of a definite kind.

For example, we know through our sensations what particular objects of various kinds look like—what particular trees look like, let us say. A word, such as " tree ", then refers in general to things which look like that.

Hence by means of words we can express general conclusions about things and their properties, and about how they are to be used. For example, a group of men interested in cutting down trees can represent to themselves by words the methods which they will employ, and so plan and co-ordinate their social labour. And once possessed of the signal system of speech, they can go much further than this into the sphere of generalisation—distinguishing, for example, the different properties of trees, and the general conditions of their growth.

The use of words arises, as we have said, in the social activity of man, as a product and instrument, in the first place, of social labour. From the very beginning it serves as a medium of human social communication. The second signal system, from which comes the use of words, does not and could not arise and develop as the personal or private possession of individuals, each of whom uses it for his own purposes without relation to other individuals. On the contrary, it arises because, from the beginnings of human social activity, men need to communicate general ideas and conclusions to one another—and so they evolve the means of doing this.

The second signal system, therefore, can arise and develop only by the formation of a *language*, common to a social group.

In the first place, there must be words whose constant reference has become fixed in their common use by a social group. In the second place, there must also be conventions fixed by the same common use governing the ways in which words are combined together.

A language is characterised, first, by its basic stock of words, and second, by its grammar. Grammar " determines the rules governing the modification of words and the combination of words into sentences, and thus lends coherence and meaning to language. . . . The grammatical system of a language and its basic word stock constitute its foundation, the specific nature of the language."[1]

Development of Language and of Thought

It is when men begin to use tools for social production that they also begin to speak and to evolve a language, and thereby to form ideas about the surrounding world. It was " from and in the process of labour " that language originated. And this origin explains the essential, elementary features of language

[1] Stalin, *Concerning Marxism in Linguistics*

as an instrument for communication and exchange of thoughts.

Language, which thus originates in man's productive activity, and directly serves that productive activity, of necessity further serves the whole of the human social intercourse and activity that develops along with and on the basis of production.

"Language", wrote Stalin, "is connected with man's productive activity directly, and not only with man's productive activity, but with all his other activity. . . .

"Language is a medium, an instrument with the help of which people communicate with one another, exchange thoughts and understand each other. . . . Without it, it is impossible to ensure the success of society's productive activity, and hence the very existence of social production becomes impossible. Consequently, without a language understood by a society and common to all its members, that society must cease to produce, must disintegrate and cease to exist as a society. In this sense, language, while it is a medium of intercourse, is at the same time an instrument of struggle and development of society. . . .

"Language serves society as a means of intercourse between people, as a means of exchanging thoughts in society, as a means enabling people to understand each other and to organise joint work in all spheres of human activity, both in the sphere of production and in the sphere of economic relations, in the sphere of politics and in the sphere of culture, in social and everyday life."[1]

A language, therefore, is always the common language of a whole people and develops continuously throughout the whole history of a people.

"Language is one of those social phenomena which operate throughout the existence of a society. It arises and develops with the rise and development of a society. It dies when the society dies. . . . Language and its laws of development can be understood only if studied in inseparable connection with the history of society, with the history of the people to whom the language under study belongs, and who are its creators and repositories."[2]

[1] Ibid.   [2] Ibid.

When, therefore, certain would-be Marxists maintained that language develops as part of the social superstructure, Stalin emphasised that language is in no sense a part of the superstructure.

The social superstructure is essentially a product of a given system of production relations : it serves the consolidation and development of its particular economic basis, and disappears when that basis disappears. It reflects the economic relations of society and is only indirectly connected with production.

A language, on the other hand, is not the product of any particular system of economic relations. It does not serve any particular economic system and disappear when that system disappears. And it is directly connected with the development of men's productive activities.

A language is never the exclusive product or possession of any particular class. Language arises, in the first place, in men's productive activity ; and a particular language serves a particular people as their means of social intercourse, as their means of communication in their productive and all other activity. It serves as a means of communication between the different classes into which a people is divided. Under whatever economic system a people may live, their language serves alike the activity of consolidating and defending that economic system, and also of changing it and replacing it by another.

Languages develop as people's productive activity develops. They enrich and slowly change their basic word stock, and slowly modify their grammar. Different languages develop with different peoples and with the intercourse between different peoples. Thus several languages branch off from a common beginning ; languages modify one another through mutual influence, and new languages are formed through the coming together of old languages. When one people oppresses another, the language of the oppressed may likewise be stifled in its development. And when one people destroys another, they may likewise destroy the other's language.

It is important, therefore, not to confuse language with

culture ; for the same language—adding to and modifying its word stock and much more slowly modifying its grammar—in its development serves a given people throughout a series of basic changes in their culture. Thus, for example, we speak of socialist culture as being " socialist in content and national in form, i.e., in language ", since the same national language serves both the old bourgeois and the new socialist culture. " Culture changes in content with every new period in the development of society, whereas language remains basically the same through a number of periods, equally serving both the new culture and the old."[1]

It is likewise important not to confuse the development of language with the development of the views expressed in language. In the course of social development, different classes acquire different views ; the dominant views of society change from epoch to epoch, and correspond to the character of the economic system. Naturally, these views are expressed in language. But while the views differ and change, the language does not change. In expressing their peculiar class outlook, the members of a class may, of course, employ certain words and turns of phrase peculiar to themselves, just as they often have their own peculiar accent. But they do not develop a different language, with a different basic vocabulary and grammar. Different and contradictory views are all expressed in the same language, and the views which it is used to express are indifferent to the development of language.

Unlike the language in which they are expressed, the views of society are products of a particular epoch, of a particular system of production relations, of particular classes. The language in which they are expressed develops slowly through a number of epochs, by modifying its vocabulary and grammar. It develops without undergoing sudden and revolutionary changes. The views expressed in language, on the other hand, do undergo fundamental changes when a given stage of development of society is passed, when the production relations are changed, when new classes come to the fore.

[1] *Ibid.*

Can there be Thought without Language?

The study of the nature—the material basis, the functions and the laws of development—of thought and language leads to the conclusion that the formation of ideas and the exchange of ideas are impossible without language, and that ideas only take shape and develop through the means of language.

Ideas are formed and take shape only through words and the combination of words. It is by means of words and the combination of words in sentences that reality is reproduced in thoughts. Thoughts only become definite thoughts in so far as they are "registered and fixed in words and in words combined into sentences". Ideas without language are as non-existent as spirits without bodies.

Does this mean that to think is the same thing as to utter words, and that the process of thinking is a process of " talking to oneself " ? No. For in the first place, it is possible to utter words and sentences without meaning anything by them. And in the second place, once one has learned the uses of language many processes of thought can be performed without actually uttering, either aloud or " to oneself ", all the words and sentences whose use would be needed for the full enunciation of the thoughts involved.

It is well known, for example, that with people who have often discussed some subject together a few words are enough for them mutually to understand some very complex point, which it would take many words for them to explain to an outsider. This is because they have been through their explanations together earlier, and these few words recall all those explanations.

It is very much the same with thought processes in an individual brain. One can come to conclusions without the intervention of elaborate processes of inner verbalisation. But at the same time, a man deceives himself if he supposes that he has ideas of things for which he lacks words, or that he has thoughts which he is unable to express in language.

" It is said that thoughts arise in the mind of man prior to being expressed in speech, that they arise without language material, without the language shell, in, so to say, a naked form," wrote Stalin. " But this is absolutely wrong. Whatever the thoughts that may arise in the mind of man, they can arise and exist only on the basis of the language material, on the basis of language terminology and phrases. Bare thoughts, free from the language material . . . do not exist. ' Language is the direct reality of thought ', said Marx. The reality of thought manifests itself in language. Only idealists can speak . . . of thinking without language."[1]

Of course, this does not mean that there is no distinction between an idea and some particular word or phrase. It means that ideas only exist as embodied in particular words or phrases, which are used to express ideas. Ideas have no separate disembodied existence apart from their expression.

For example, the English word " red " and the French word " rouge " both express the same idea of a colour. So the idea cannot be identified with either word. But the idea of colour no more exists apart from words in which it is expressed, than colour exists apart from particular coloured objects. What makes the two words expressive of the same idea is that they have the same significance in the respective languages—that is, the two words play similar parts in elaborating through language connections between man and the external world. The thinking activity of the brain consists in nothing but such elaboration of connections with the external world ; and this is done not prior to language, nor apart from language, but precisely and only by means of language.

Language Conventions and What They Express

A feature of language is its apparently arbitrary or conventional character. A particular sound is used for a particular purpose in a language—but some other sound would have done equally well and is, perhaps, used for that very same purpose in some other language.

The discovery that words are in this way arbitrary or conventional signs was an important discovery in science,

[1] *Ibid.*

obvious as it may seem. For it used often to be believed—
and some people still believe it today—that a particular word
is in some mysterious way " the right word " for a particular
thing, and that words are connected with things by some
internal tie, and not merely by the conventions of language.

The ancient conception of a secret tie between words and
things was bound up with magic and religion. Thus it was
thought that each man had a name which was peculiarly his
own and that no other name for him could fit. His " real name "
was then often kept a secret, for it was believed that if his
enemies knew it, then they could curse his name and so do
him an injury. Similarly, the names of gods were believed
to be among the essential properties of the gods. And similarly
with other words, besides proper names. Thus there was an
old proverb which stated, " The Divine is rightly so called " :
this expressed the idea that there was something peculiarly
divine about the word " divine ".[1] To this day, some English
visitors who take a trip to France believe that the inhabitants
of that country do not know the right words for things.

But not only is the vocabulary of a language conventional,
its grammatical rules are conventional too. For different
languages employ different grammatical rules. Thus the rules
of the Chinese language, for example, are entirely different
from those of any European language ; the rules of English
are different from those of Latin or Slavonic languages ; and
the rules of what we are pleased to call " primitive " languages
are again different from them all. Nevertheless, the same
propositions can be stated in all these languages, and any one
can be translated into any other. This shows that not only
vocabulary but grammar is a conventional feature of languages.

The particular sounds which constitute the words in a given
language, and the particular rules of its grammar, are, then,
conventional. They are conventional in the sense that these
particular sounds and rules come to be used by a particular
people for historical reasons, whereas the same thoughts could

[1] Quoted by C. K. Ogden and I. A. Richards, *The Meaning of
Meaning*, London, 1946.

equally well be expressed by different sounds and different rules, such as are employed by the historically evolved languages of other peoples. But they are not, of course, conventional in the sense that they were ever resolved upon and fixed by some linguistic decision of the people concerned. In general, linguistic conventions are formed by an unconscious process in the lives of peoples. Only at a late stage are they recorded in dictionaries and grammars and do people begin consciously and deliberately to record and fix the conventions of their language.

But while both vocabulary and grammar are in the above sense conventional, nevertheless what words a language possesses, in the sense of the objects denoted by its vocabulary, is not conventional, but is determined by the objective conditions and requirements of life of the people using the language.

For example, whatever sounds are used for the purpose, a language must have words for all the things, properties, relations, etc., which are of practical importance in the life of the people. In general, the higher the stage of development of production the greater is necessarily the basic word stock of language.

Similarly, the relations and connections among things and people which are expressed by combining words into sentences according to the rules of grammar are not conventional either, but are determined by what has to be reflected in sentences.

For example, whatever the grammar of a language is, it must have conventions for expressing the action of one thing on another, the connection between a thing and its different or changing properties, and so on. Different languages employ different grammatical conventions for expressing propositions, but those conventions must all satisfy the same requirements arising from what has to be expressed, which is common to all languages.

Hence while people fix the conventions of their language, both as regards its word stock and its grammar, those conventions express objective requirements common to every language, and must always satisfy those same requirements.

Language and Logic

Language is "directly connected with thought, language registers and fixes in words, and in words combined into sentences, the results of thought and man's successes in his quest for knowledge".[1]

Whatever the results of thought which are to be expressed, and whatever language they are expressed in, they must satisfy the basic requirements of the reflection of reality in thought. These requirements give rise to laws of thought, to principles of logic. For thoughts are reflections of the real world, and in the process of reflection, as Marx said, the material world is translated into forms of thought. This process of reflection and translation has its own necessary laws—the laws of thought, the principles of logic.

The laws of thought involve, in the first place, the logical principles for constructing significant propositions.

There are, for example, simple propositions and compound propositions. The construction of simple propositions involves such logical operations as affirmation, negation, relation and so on; and compound propositions are constructed by combining simple propositions through such logical operations as we express by words like "and", "or", "if . . . then", and so on. Thus, "This is red", "This is not red", "This is getting red", "This is redder than that", are all simple propositions. And "This is red and that is green", "Either this is red or I am colour blind", and "If this is red then it will soon be green", are compound propositions. The construction of all such propositions involves definite logical principles—that is to say, principles of how the terms may be combined into significant propositions.

The laws of thought involve, in the second place, the logical principles for determining which propositions logically follow from other propositions and which are logically incompatible with them. These are the principles which we use in argument and reasoning.

For example, " If all A is B, and all B is C, then all A is C".

[1] Stalin *loc. cit.*

This is a general logical principle, which tells us that the third proposition logically follows from the first two.[1]

Such a principle, of course, contains no guarantee as to the truth of propositions : it is concerned with their logical relations with one another, not with their truth. Thus it tells us that if we have discovered that the first two propositions are true, then we need no further investigation to assure ourselves of the truth of the third, for it follows from the first two. But if the first two propositions are in fact untrue, then, though the third proposition follows from them, it may be true or it may be false. Logic by itself tells us nothing about the truth of propositions, which can be discovered and verified only by empirical investigation.

Another example of a logical principle is the principle of non-contradiction, which was originally stated by Aristotle as follows : " The same attribute cannot at the same time belong and not belong to the same subject in the same respect."[2] This is a general logical principle which tells us that some propositions are logically incompatible with others. Contradictory positions cannot be consistently combined together.

[1] This particular principle was originally formulated by Aristotle, who called it " the first figure of the syllogism". See *First Analytics*, Book I, ch. 4.

[2] Aristotle, *Metaphysics*, Book IV, ch. 3. Having included the words " at the same time, in the same respect ", he further observed : " We must presuppose, in face of dialectical objections, any further qualifications which might be added."

Many " dialectical objections " have been made since then to the logical principle of non-contradiction. And formulations made later by the Scholastics and repeated by modern logicians, which stupidly left out the original qualifications made by Aristotle (himself a dialectician), are wide open to such objections.

Thus the principle has been expressed : " A cannot be both A and not A." Such a formulation is absurd, since it is evident that if things exist only in interconnection and motion, then a thing can very well manifest some characteristic only in certain respects and relations, and not in others. And it is equally evident that if a thing is in process of change, then it may be impossible either to affirm or to deny that it has some fixed characteristic.

Many crude and mistaken formulations of logical principles

All such logical principles are precisely laws of thought, not laws of reality : they are not the laws of material processes, but the laws of the reflection of material processes. And because they are requirements of the reflection of ‚reality in thought, arising from the very nature of the form of the reflection as it has developed in the course of human practice, the laws of logic require to be satisfied in the working out and expression of views. If our thoughts violate the laws of logic, then they become incoherent and self-contradictory.

This accounts for what is sometimes called the " normative " character of the laws of logic, and for their character of " logical " as opposed to " natural " necessity. Our thoughts need not be logical, but unless they are they cannot satisfy the requirements of the reflection of reality : this is why the laws of logic constitute a " norm " for thought. And the laws of logic arise from the very nature of thought, quite independent of the particular object of thought : this is why the laws of logic have a self-evident and axiomatic character, as distinct from the laws of nature, which have to be discovered through an empirical investigation of external reality.

So whatever the views which are being worked out in society, they are all subordinate to the same laws of thought, to the same principles of logic. Just as the same language is used

have been written down by people with a metaphysical rather than a dialectical approach—though it is worth nothing that Aristotle, on whom such mistakes are often blamed, was careful not to make them. Dialectics teaches us to correct such mistakes. But dialectics does not thereby go against or change the principles of logic. The aim of the dialectical method is to enable us logically and consistently to express the real interconnection and motion of things.

People with a metaphysical approach try to express changing things in fixed categories, and try to express the relations of things in categories suited only to considering things in separation. As a result, they are often landed in contradictions. Just as when a motor car splutters we know there is something wrong with the engine, so when a philosopher contradicts himself we know there is something wrong with his ideas. Dialectics enables us to keep clear of logical contradictions, and to be absolutely consistent. Hence dialectics always respects the logical principle of non-contradiction, although meta-physics frequently violates it.

to express different views, so do different views employ the same laws of thought, the same logic.

New views do not, therefore, give rise to a new logic, any more than they give rise to a new language. On the contrary, the principles of logic are inherent in the very process of thought and of its expression in language, and are not altered with alterations of views.

Some people, of course, ignore logic in the working out of their views. So much the worse for their views. This does not mean that they have evolved a different logic, but rather that they fail to be logical.

No discussion, no controversy or argument, no development of thought whatever would be possible, if the laws of thought changed and were different for different people. Anyone who thinks that the laws of thought change, that different epochs have a different logic, thereby denies the very possibility of thought as a reflection of objective reality. Logic arises from the universal requirements of the reflection of reality in thought, and not from the particular interests which particular processes of thought may serve from time to time.

Marxist materialism, therefore, denies that logic is a super-structure, just as it denies that language is a superstructure. Language is the means of expression and communication of thought, and logic consists of the laws of thought. They are therefore inseparably connected, since language is " the direct reality of thought ", and the laws of thought necessarily express themselves in and impose themselves upon the development and use of language. Language and logic are employed in-differently for the working out and expression of any views, whatever the basis of such views.

Hence if, for example, a socialist is arguing with a defender of capitalism, they both appeal to and try to base their arguments on the same principles of logic, just as they both speak the same language. Just as " two plus two equals four " for the accountant of a capitalist or of a socialist enterprise, so " if all A is B, then some A is B " for a defender of socialism or of capitalism. Similarly, anyone who has read accounts of the labours of Christian missionaries among primitive peoples will realise that both parties to the argument appeal to the same laws of logic, though it must be confessed that the primitive people are often more logical than the missionaries.

What is here said about logic does not, however, apply to the philosophical views expounded by those who have written books about logic. Those philosophical views, often labelled "Logic", are, of course, the views of particular classes and of particular epochs, and constitute part of a social superstructure.

Thus we conclude that language develops as the means of expressing and communicating thoughts by people in society, arising from and developed in the course of their productive activity and all their other social activity ; and that the thoughts of men, expressed in language, are subordinate to logic, to the laws of thought as reflection of material reality. At the same time, the social views which are expressed in language and worked out with the aid of logic develop on the basis of men's economic relations, of the activities and interests of social classes.

Part Two

THE DEVELOPMENT OF IDEAS

CHAPTER FIVE

ABSTRACT IDEAS

In thinking we proceed from elementary ideas, to which correspond objects directly perceptible to the senses, to abstract ideas. Abstract ideas have their source in the development of social relationships and of productive and other activities concerned with external nature, while men's ignorance and helplessness give rise to the formation of mystical and illusory abstract ideas. With abstract ideas begins the division of mental from material labour, and then the divorce of theoretical from practical activity, with the tendency of theory to fly away from reality. From this also stems the opposition between the idealist and materialist trends in thinking.

The Formation of Abstract Ideas

WHILE thought and ideas, like language, originate from labour, men likewise develop their thinking and their ideas in the course of the whole of their social activity.

Writing of the development of ideas or of human consciousness—for the peculiarity of human consciousness is that man is conscious of things not only through perceptions but also through ideas—Marx and Engels showed that man's consciousness arises and develops " only from the need, the necessity, of intercourse with other men. . . . Consciousness is therefore from the very beginning a social product, and remains so as long as men exist at all."[1]

Ideas are not the products of a pure intellectual process, nor are they mere automatic responses to stimuli reaching us from external objects. They are produced by human brains in the course of human social activity. They reflect the connections of men with one another and with the external world, the real conditions of men's existence.

Marx and Engels went on to point out that " consciousness

[1] Marx and Engels, *The German Ideology*, Part I, ch. 1.

is at first merely consciousness concerning the immediate sensuous environment and consciousness of the limited connections with other persons and things. . . . This beginning", they added, " is as animal as social life itself at this stage. It is mere herd consciousness."[1]

The first and most elementary ideas are ideas directly derived from immediate practical intercourse with other people and surrounding objects. They are formed by giving names to the common features of things recognisable in perception. From the start, as Marx has stressed, " the production of ideas " arises from " the material activity and material intercourse of men". And out of this activity and material intercourse at its most elementary level is already formed a complex of elementary ideas of external objects, of the self and of other people—of the kinds and properties of objects and their various connections with and uses for people.

In such ideas are more or less directly reflected the salient features of objects and human activities as we are immediately aware of them in perception. Such ideas constitute the basic, elementary equipment of human thought and communication. They are expressed in words denoting familiar objects, and properties and relations of objects, and everyday activities.

We all possess a rich equipment of such ideas. Our possession of them represents a considerable social achievement, but we take them quite for granted, use them all the time, and every child learns them at an early age. Such are our ideas of the things about us with which our normal affairs are concerned, such as men and women, tables, chairs, motor cars, trees, flowers, dogs, cats, etc., etc. ; of sensible properties of things, such as red, blue, hard, soft, big, small, and so on ; and of actions and relations, such as running, walking, falling, above, below, etc., etc. Our own equipment of elementary ideas is obviously far greater than that of primitive man, precisely because we do many more things and concern ourselves with many more objects and relations. Nevertheless, the consciousness represented by such elementary ideas remains, as Marx

[1] *Ibid.*

and Engels put it, "consciousness concerning the immediate sensuous environment and consciousness of the limited connections with other persons and things".

The feature of all such elementary ideas is that they have a concrete, sensuous content, because to them correspond objects directly perceptible to the senses. The development of social intercourse, however, leads to the formation of more abstract ideas, to which no directly perceptible object corresponds.

Can we form such ideas, to which no directly perceptible object corresponds? Yes, of course we can, and we do. For example, men are directly perceptible objects, and their properties of being tall, short, thin, fat, and so on, are directly perceptible properties. But we also think of men in other terms than these, although nothing directly evident to the senses corresponds to what we think about them. If I see a very fat man and say, "He's a bloated capitalist", his perceptible fatness corresponds to the word "bloated", but no corresponding perceptible property corresponds to the word "capitalist". Nevertheless, the ideas of "capitalist" and "capitalism" are well thought-out, well established ideas. They are abstract ideas, to which no directly perceptible object corresponds. We are, in fact, continually employing an enormous range of such abstract ideas. All kinds of social and legal ideas, moral ideas, religious ideas, scientific ideas, philosophical ideas—they are all abstract, in the sense we are now discussing.

Our ideas, then, are not in their development confined to the reflection of the common features of external objects presented to the senses. Ideas are always formed according to the needs of social intercourse. And with the development of production and the consequent development of production relations, and of social relations and social activity generally, ideas are developed beyond the limited stage of consciousness of the common features of objects perceived through the senses. Men form general concepts and views about the world and their own social life. Such more abstract ideas are formed in men's minds as a product of their active relationship to external nature and to one another, and serve the development of social intercourse based on those relationships. But no directly perceptible objects correspond to them.

It is to such ideas that we shall now apply the term " abstract ideas ", contrasting the degree of abstraction which they represent with the relative concreteness of other ideas.

The Stages of Abstraction

We stated at the end of Chapter One that words are used to pick out, to abstract and generalise, what is common between different sensations. It is important to note that in this sense all ideas without exception are abstract, since the very process of forming ideas is a process of abstraction. When, therefore, we apply the term " abstract " to distinguish certain ideas from others, we use this term only in a relative sense, meaning that one idea is more abstract than another, or rather, represents a higher level of abstraction.

Indeed, not merely ideas but perceptions too involve abstraction. The very process of reflection of material reality in consciousness is a process of abstraction, since what is reflected is not, and cannot be, the whole of the concrete material reality presented, but only aspects of it. The only *absolute* distinction which can be drawn between the abstract and the concrete is the distinction between the concreteness of material reality and the abstractness of its reflection in consciousness.

Sense-perception involves an abstraction from concrete reality, since when we perceive a thing only certain aspects of it are reflected in our sensations. For example, when I look at a chair before sitting on it, I see only a part of the surface of the chair. At the same time, sense-perceptions may be said to be concrete in comparison with the abstractness of ideas, since sensations are signals of particular, concrete objects, whereas ideas are formed by a further process of abstraction. The idea of a chair, for example, is an abstraction formed out of the repeated perception of particular chairs, and expresses what is common to many particulars. The abstraction involved in ideas is, therefore, of another order from that involved in perception. Perception involves the abstraction of particular aspects of a thing from the concrete thing, whereas ideas abstract what is common from among many particulars. Thus, again, the idea of " furniture " is more abstract than the idea of a particular kind of furniture, such as a chair. And the idea of a " thing " or of a " body " is more abstract still.

But a further process of abstraction enters into the formation of ideas. When we abstract from particulars what is common to them, it is still the case that directly perceptible objects correspond to our ideas. We can illustrate what we mean by a chair, or by a piece of furniture, or by a body, by pointing to particular chairs, pieces of furniture or bodies as the perceptible objects corresponding to our ideas. But a new level of abstraction is reached when we form ideas to which no perceptible object corresponds. Thus I can tell you what I mean by " a man " by drawing your attention to men, but if I want to tell you what I mean by " the rights of man ", a complicated explanation of a different kind is required.

There are, then, two levels or stages of abstraction in the development of ideas ; and thought, in its development, passes on from the first stage to the second. The first stage arises when, out of sense experience, we form ideas of the different kinds of objects, their properties, relations and motions, perceptible by the senses. The second stage arises when, by a new process of abstraction, we form ideas of the properties, relations and motions of things which are not directly perceptible by the senses.

The Sources of Abstract Ideas

All abstract ideas, without exception, have their source through experience in the objective material world, in men's practical relations with things and with one another. For it is definite experiences of men, derived from their intercourse with one another and with nature, which lead them to form abstract ideas. These ideas serve the continuance and development of that intercourse. And they reflect definite relations objectively existing between things, between men, and between men and things, which are translated in the minds of men into terms of abstract ideas.

One important source of the development of abstract ideas is the development of social relationships between people. Thus, for example, the primitive gentile organisation of society—with its complicated rules about who can marry whom, who belongs to what gens, and, in general, who can do what—gives rise to a whole set of abstract ideas about social relationships, which are at once the products of those social relationships and their regulators. Later, ideas of social status, chieftainship and so on arise. And later, with the development of property, abstract ideas connected with property relations.

For example, when certain people have taken possession of the land, then there are formed ideas of landownership and of corresponding duties, rights and privileges. Such ideas of ownership are abstract ideas, to which corresponds no object immediately perceptible to the senses. Thus the idea of a ploughed field, say, is the idea of a reality presented to our senses ; but the idea of the ownership of that field is an abstract idea to which no directly perceptible object corresponds. Similarly, the produce of that field is a concrete, perceptible reality—we can eat it, for example ; but the right of the land-owner to take possession of that product is not perceptible. But these abstract ideas are the ideal reflection of something real and objective—the production relations established at a definite stage of the evolution of social production.

Other abstract ideas are formed as a consequence of the development of men's productive and other activities concerned with external nature. For example, this is the source of such abstract ideas as those of cause and effect, and, again, of all the abstract ideas concerned with counting and measuring, such as those of number, space and time.

One very important influence in the development of men's abstract ideas is their relative ignorance and helplessness in the midst of their social activities. This starts off the development of all kinds of mystical and illusory abstract ideas.

At a very early stage of society people begin to think about the underlying causes which operate in the various processes with which they are familiar and on which they depend for their livelihood. Thus, for example, people see the crops growing or the animals multiplying, and they are aware of what they themselves have to do to promote these processes. But they do not see and are not aware of the underlying causes which operate in these processes, nor have they any but most inadequate means of controlling them. And so they begin to form the concepts of unseen powers. Most primitive peoples have the concept of a secret power residing in men, animals and things, which they regard as something not perceptible to the senses which nevertheless penetrates and controls all sensible things. Thus certain Red Indian tribes called this power *wakanda*, and one of their elders, trying to explain the idea to a visiting anthropologist, told him : " No man has ever seen *wakanda*."[1] From this type of abstract idea—the idea of unseen powers—develop the abstract ideas of religion and theology.

Division of Mental from Material Labour

Abstract ideas are formed, as we can see from these few examples, as a consequence of the process of social development. And Marx and Engels connected the development of abstract ideas with the fundamental social process of division of labour.

The formation of all abstract ideas—of whatever type, and whatever the particular source of the ideas—presupposes a certain development of men's productive powers and social relations. It therefore presupposes a certain division of labour. This division of labour begins to separate the single productive group or " herd " into distinct individuals—distinct not merely as different members of the species but as persons with distinct social functions and positions, with individuality. This gives rise to the activities, relations and experiences from which the formation of abstract ideas arises. And it likewise brings to

[1] Quoted from A. Robertson, *The Origins of Christianity*, p. 12. London, 1953.

an end the stage of " herd " consciousness, and permits the development of individual thought.

With the formation of abstract ideas, a division of mental from material labour appears. It marks a definite beginning of mental as distinct from material labour. And with this, there begin to appear wise men, elders and leaders of various kinds who are the specialists in ideas and who expound and develop them. This specialisation in ideas develops as an indispensable feature of social life ; for without ideas, division of labour and the various consequent productive processes and social relations cannot be maintained or developed. And so Marx and Engels observed : " Division of labour only becomes truly such from the moment when a division of mental and material labour appears."[1]

In general, the formation of abstract ideas corresponds to new social needs arising. At the same time, the development of ideas becomes a special form of social activity, a special department of the division of labour. And the ensuing separation of mental from material labour then leads to further consequences.

Once an abstract idea is formed and embodied in words, then the possibility arises that these words will be taken to refer to special kinds of objects which exist apart from the objects of the material world which are reflected in sense-perceptions. And this possibility is the more apt to be realised, the more the handling of abstract ideas becomes a special social activity separated from material labour.

It is obvious that precisely this takes place with concepts of unseen powers, supernatural beings, and so on. The people who employ these abstract ideas consider that certain mysterious beings and powers, whose existence is separate from and independent of the existence of perceptible, material things, correspond to the ideas. And the witch doctors, priests or theologians who specialise in such ideas work out the most elaborate doctrines in terms of them.

But similar illusions can grow up around all abstract ideas. Abstract ideas are such that no directly perceptible object

[1] Marx and Engels, *loc. cit.*

corresponds to them. But they do relate to perceptible objects. To explain an abstract idea, to say what the abstract word in which it is embodied means, it is necessary to refer to definite perceptible objects and processes and their relationships which are reflected in the abstract idea. On the other hand, it is possible to forget about the concrete reality which is reflected in abstract ideas, and to manipulate such ideas as though they dealt with some separate realm of abstractions revealed to the intellect but independent of the perceptible world of experience and practice.

" The approach of the mind to a particular thing, the taking of a cast of it," wrote Lenin, " is not a simple, direct act, a lifeless mirror reflection, but a complex, twofold, zig-zag act, which harbours the possibility that the fantasy may entirely fly away from reality. What is more, it harbours the possibility that the abstract idea may be transformed, imperceptibly and unwittingly, into fantasy—and in the long run, into God. For even the simplest generalisation and the most elementary general idea is a fragment of fantasy."[1]

This " flying away " of the abstract idea from reality is the more apt to take place, the more mental labour is divorced from material labour, the more theoretical activity is divorced from practical activity.

With the development of abstract ideas, then, thinking is no longer tied down to the features of things and the connections of persons and things of which we are immediately aware in practice through the senses. And just because thinking becomes the special province of mental as distinct from material labour, all the more does it cut loose from the practice and the experiences of ordinary working life. It becomes free to elaborate all manner of general concepts and general views about the world and about society. What we think becomes distinct from what we experience or perceive.

" From this moment onwards," wrote Marx and Engels, " consciousness can really flatter itself that it is something other than consciousness of existing practice, that it is really

[1] Lenin, *Philosophical Notebooks*.

conceiving something without conceiving something real [i.e., something directly perceptible to the senses—M.C.]. From now on, consciousness is in a position to emancipate itself from the world and to proceed to the formation of ' pure ' theory, theology, philosophy, ethics, etc."[1]

Learning How to Think

A condition for the development of abstract ideas is the separation of mental from material labour. And it contains within itself contradictory potentialities. On the one hand, it permits the acquisition of profounder knowledge of the real connections of things and of the conditions of human existence than is contained in immediate perceptual consciousness. On the other hand, it permits the growth of all kinds of fantasies and illusions.

Consequently the whole process of the intellectual development of society presents contradictory aspects. On the one hand, there has been the undoubted growth of genuine knowledge, in other words, of true ideas, whose correspondence with reality has been verified, concerning nature, society and the relations of men with nature. On the other hand, there has been the growth and elaboration of illusory ideas. As society has developed, so men have developed in their minds illusions about themselves and the world they inhabit. Each epoch has added to the sum total of human knowledge. And at the same time, each epoch has produced its characteristic illusions, which circumscribed, penetrated and coloured the entire intellectual production of that epoch.

It is here, then, that we find the root of the opposition and struggle of materialist and idealist tendencies which has run right through the whole development of thought.

The opposition of materialist and idealist tendencies is a fundamental opposition, arising from the very nature of thought itself, once it has developed to the level of abstract ideas. It arises with the separation of mental from material labour. When mental labour first begins to " emancipate itself from the

[1] Marx and Engels, *loc. cit.*

world " as a theoretical activity, and to " become something other than existing practice ", then there immediately arise the two alternative paths of theory—to strive to understand things in their own connections and to explain what happens in the material world from the material world itself, which is materialism ; or to launch out into the realm of pure thought and represent the material, sensuous world as dependent on thought and the product of thought, which is idealism. In other words, to regard being as prior to thinking, or thinking as prior to being.

Understood in this light, the struggle of the materialist tendency in thought against the idealist tendency is understood as a struggle, carried forward through ages of human history from primitive times up to the present day and into the future, to learn to think truthfully and correctly, in a way that truthfully reflects the real conditions of human existence and helps human progress. It is the struggle for knowledge and enlightenment against ignorance and superstition.

CHAPTER SIX

IDEOLOGY

Abstract ideas are used in the elaboration of more or less
systematic views about things, or ideologies, which are evolved
by definite social groups in definite stages of social development. Ideological development depends on the development
of the material life of society, and ideologies serve class interests.
At the same time, ideologies must always be made to satisfy
certain intellectual requirements. Hence arise continual contradictions in ideological development, and the criticism of
ideologies. Hence elements of both truth and illusion co-exist
in ideologies.

The Formation of Ideologies

IN the course of the development of society abstract ideas
are used for the elaboration of more or less systematic
theories, doctrines or views about things. General views and
ways of thinking, systems of abstract ideas, become established
as characteristic of the outlook of a whole society, or of a section
of society.

And considerable differences exist between the views entertained in different societies and in different stages of social
development. Each possesses its typical social views of politics,
morality, law, property, religion, philosophy—and these views
penetrate social thinking on all particular topics, and mould
and influence the development of ideas of all individuals.

With the development of private property and the state, for
example, abstract ideas about legal and political " rights " are
always formed. But in different stages of the development of
property, the views which are held about rights—the theories
which are entertained about them, the systematic doctrines
about rights—vary considerably. In slave society, slaves were
thought to have no rights whatever. In feudal society, everyone
was thought to have rights, but the character of his rights

depended on his actual position in the feudal order, so that the rights of a serf were not equal to those of a lord. With the rise of capitalism, the theory of " human rights " began to be formed—the view that every man, simply as a human being, possesses certain " inalienable human rights " which are the same for all men—and there has been a great deal of argument as to the exact definition of these rights and from what they may be deduced.

Again, from the very beginnings of social production people have formed abstract ideas about the causal processes in nature. But in different stages of society the views about causality in nature have varied considerably. The most primitive theory is the theory of animism, which thinks of everything as though it were alive and conscious. Later on, animism is given up, and everything is thought to be directed by its specific form or principle, which determines its nature, its place in the hierarchy of being and its peculiar ways of acting on other things and reacting to them. This view of causality was elaborated in great detail during the Middle Ages. Then again there has developed the mechanistic view of causality which was characteristic in its beginnings of modern natural science, according to which the motions of all bodies are governed by a single set of natural laws and everything that happens is determined by the external interactions of bodies taking place in accordance with these laws.

Such more or less systematic views, which are historically evolved by definite social groups in definite stages of social development, and which vary according to their social origin, are called *ideologies*. And the development of such views is called *ideological development*.

The Material Basis of Ideological Development

Ideology is essentially a social rather than an individual product. In dealing with the development of ideology, we are dealing with the social development of ideas. We are not so much concerned with how ideas are formed and elaborated in the mind of the individual, as with how broad currents of ideas are formed as characteristic of a whole phase of social development.

Of course, individuals contribute as individuals, according to their capacities and circumstances, to the formation of ideologies. On the other hand, the ideologies prevailing or rising in society always constitute the background and condition for the development of the opinions and views of every individual in society. Individuals, in their own opinions and views, are always influenced by the ideologies, express them, are their mouthpieces.

In the course of social development there is change and development of ideology. One ideology supplants another. And in the same society, different and rival ideologies interact and clash with one another. But ideology has no independent development. There is no " history of thought ", independent of the development of the material conditions of social life.

An ideology is always the ideology of definite people, living in definite conditions, depending for their life on a definite mode of production, with definite social relations, doing definite things with definite desires and aims. And their ideology is not formed independently of the process of their material life.

" We set out from real, active men," wrote Marx and Engels, " and on the basis of their real life process we demonstrate the development of the ideological reflexes and echoes of this life process. The phantoms formed in the human brain are also, necessarily, sublimates of their material life process, which is empirically verifiable and bound to material premises. Morality, religion, metaphysics, all the rest of ideology, and their corresponding forms of consciousness, thus no longer retain the semblance of independence. They have no history, no development ; but men, developing their material production and their material intercourse, alter, along with this their real existence, their thinking and the products of their thinking."[1]

It is the development of production, and the consequent development of production relations and of the social intercourse based on them, which give rise to the conditions for the

[1] Marx and Engels, *The German Ideology*, Part I, ch. 1.

formation of abstract ideas and to the social need for the ideological development of such ideas. Ideologies develop not as a consequence of the inner working of men's minds going on independently of the material life of society but as a consequence of the development of the material life of society, which conditions the products of intellectual production.

In class-divided society, therefore, ideologies take on a class character. Different views are developed on the basis of the different places occupied by different classes in social production, their different relationships to the means of production, their different roles in the social organisation of labour, their different ways of obtaining their share of the social wealth, their different material interests. The different ideologies are thus developed in the service of different class interests.

The Ideological Reflection of Reality

Ideological development is, then, governed by the material development of society—by the development of production, of the relations of production, and of classes and the class struggle.

Hence the causes impelling ideological development in one or another direction are always to be found, in the last analysis, not within the sphere of ideological development itself but in the sphere of the conditions of material life. To explain, for example, why the bourgeois idea of human rights supplanted the feudal idea of rights, it is necessary to consider the changes taking place in the mode of production of material life—for these changes gave rise to a contradiction between the feudal idea of rights and the actual rights the recognition of which was necessary to carry on the bourgeois mode of production, and necessitated a change in the idea of rights to correspond with reality. Similarly, in the sphere of ideas about nature, these same changes in the mode of production imparted a new direction to the development of ideas about nature. And in general, feudal ideology was supplanted by bourgeois ideology, because, in the material life of society, feudal social relations were being supplanted by bourgeois social relations.

But at the same time, ideological development, as a development of abstract thinking, has its own special characteristics, its own internal laws. Its direction is determined by the development of the material life of society, and every ideology is developed on the basis of definite material social relationships and activities in the service of definite material interests. But it remains none the less true that ideology must always satisfy certain intellectual requirements, and that these requirements are continually posed and met in the course of ideological development.

Ideologies are developed to serve definite class interests. They are intellectual instruments, intellectual weapons, made and forged by definite classes corresponding to the material position and requirements of those classes. But just because they are intellectual instruments and intellectual weapons, to be serviceable they must satisfy intellectual requirements. They must obey the rules of working with ideas, just as, for example, material instruments and material weapons must obey the rules of working with, say, metals.

From what do these internal, intellectual requirements of ideological development arise? They arise from the fact that ideology is a reflection of the real, material world in the form of abstract ideas. Every ideology is an attempt made by people to understand and give an account of the real world in which they live, or of some aspect of it and of their own lives, so that it may be of service to them in the definite conditions in which they live. Therefore they must always strive to develop their ideology as a coherent system of ideas which squares with the facts so far as they have experienced and ascertained them. This poses intellectual requirements to be satisfied by ideologies, and to satisfy them is a law which is continually at work influencing the development of ideologies.

Ideologies must be made to satisfy, in the first place, the general requirements of the reflection of reality in ideas, that is to say, the laws of logic. In the second place, they must satisfy the particular requirements of the reflection of a particular part of reality, that is to say, they must be made to square with the facts so far as people have experienced and ascertained them.

Ideologies, therefore, are developed on the basis of the given structure of society to serve the interests of one or another class, and in this ideological development the effort is always being made to render the views developed self-consistent and logical, and to make them cover and give some consistent account of the principal facts which emerge in the experience of society at the given stage of development.

This gives rise to continual contradictions in the development of ideologies. For on the one hand, the views developed by the representatives of various classes prove logically inconsistent and inconsistent with plain facts ; and on the other hand, facts and the requirements of logic lead to conclusions which do not accord with views tenaciously held. Such contradictions give rise to a continual process of the elaboration of ideologies, as the ideologists endeavour to find ways and means of resolving them.

The Criticism of Ideologies

No matter what field of ideas is in question, the development of ideas expresses the effort to argue them out, make them consistent, present them logically, and adapt them to the facts of experience. And this effort plays a major part in the detailed elaboration of ideologies. Indeed, the more concretely we study the development of particular ideologies—that is to say, the more we study their development in detail, rather than confining attention to their most general features—the more is it necessary to take into account the intellectual aspect of ideological development. For the effort to square up ideas with obtrusive facts, and to eliminate contradictions and present a consistent, argued case, influences very greatly the real development of ideas. And in the course of this development, it inevitably happens that the expression of economic relations and class interests in the given field of ideas becomes less obvious, less direct, more obscure and roundabout.

Thus Engels wrote, for instance, of the development of legal ideology :

" Law must not only correspond to the general economic condition and be its expression, but must also be an *internally coherent* expression which does not, owing to inner contradictions, reduce itself to nought. And in order to achieve this, the faithful reflection of economic conditions suffers increasingly. . . . Thus to a great extent the course of the ' development of right ' [i.e., the development of legal ideology—M.C.] only consists, first, in the attempt to do away with the contradictions arising from the direct translation of economic relations into legal principles and to establish a harmonious system of law, and then in the repeated breaches made in this system by the influence and pressure of further economic development, which involves it in further contradictions."[1]

The same process takes place in all ideological spheres—in philosophy, theology, moral ideas, ideas about nature, and so on.

Ideologies are always peculiarly vulnerable and open to criticism on the score of self-contradiction and of failure to reckon with experienced facts. Those who, as intellectual representatives of a given class, espouse a general point of view in ideology, are always being driven for this reason to elaborate their ideology, which leads them to the creation of often very complicated and far-fetched ideological structures. Then again, as Engels observed, the structures become unsuitable for the service of the given interests in new conditions, and the process begins anew. This shows itself in philosophy, for instance, in the multiplication of " systems " of philosophy.

If this process of criticism goes on in the development of the ideology of a particular class, it takes a different and sharper form when, on the basis of new factors in the material life of society, new and rival views begin to be formed, expressing the interests of different classes. Such new views do not emerge until the development of material life gives birth to them. But once they emerge, then they attack from the new point of view the manifold inconsistencies of the already established views. They make use of logic and appeal

[1] Engels, *Letter* to C. Schmidt, October 27, 1890.

to facts as powerful intellectual weapons with which to discredit and demolish the old views.

Historians of ideas have most often erred by attempting to understand ideological development exclusively in terms of the posing and satisfaction of intellectual requirements. As Marx and Engels pointed out, that cannot be done, since one cannot say why new views should arise at particular times, or why the views should be of one rather than another type, without looking for the reasons in the material life of society. But it is also impossible to trace the development of ideologies without taking the intellectual requirements into account. And Marxism certainly never says that we should attempt to do so.

This is the opposite error into which some schools of sociologists have fallen—namely, those who embrace the doctrine of " economic determinism ", which regards economic activity as the sole agency determining the whole of social development in all its aspects. Failing to recognise that in ideology there takes place a process of the reflection of the real world in men's ideas, they regard ideology exclusively as a development of various ideas expressing and serving various material, economic interests. This leads them to one or other of two conclusions. On the one hand, they conclude that since all ideas are merely practical instruments serving various material interests, no ideas, including their own, can lay any claim correctly to reflect reality—so that every ideology, including their own, is as illusory as every other in all respects. On the other hand, they are led to make an exception of themselves and of their own ideas, representing themselves as special people who, by some intellectual miracle, have transcended every class point of view and can look down on the rest of mankind from an ivory tower of complete and absolute " objectivity ". In either case, they are clearly involved in self-contradiction.

However, there is always and always has been a basis for the criticism of ideologies in terms of reason and experience— that is to say, for their critical comparison with reality. And this comparison has been continually carried out in the course of ideological development itself. It has not been carried out by people who have managed to detach themselves from social life, for such people do not exist; but it has been carried out in the course of the long development of human practice—of production, of science and of the class struggle.

Thus in the development of ideologies there does take place a development of the truthful and coherent reflection of the real world in men's ideas. For the continuous process of reckoning with facts and striving for consistency—despite all the intellectual dishonesty, special pleading, invention, fantasy, sophism and inconsistency which accompanies it at every stage—does continuously yield positive results. And these results are continuously verified, consolidated, criticised and carried forward through the developing practice of mankind.

Truth and Illusion in Ideologies

All ideas are a reflection of objective material reality, which is their ultimate source. But while, as we have just seen, there is a development in ideology of the truthful reflection of reality in ideas, this takes place amid a development of all kinds of illusions, of distorted, fantastic reflection of reality.

The opposition and interpenetration of truth and illusion in ideological development expresses the fact that the reflection of reality in ideas is effected in different ways, through different processes, by different routes.

One way in which our ideas about things are formed and elaborated is in the process of our practical interaction with things, founded on and tested in practical experience, and further developed by scientific investigation of real processes, of the real properties of things, their motions and interconnections. In so far as ideas about things are formed in this way, the ideas and conclusions about them embodied in ideologies are more or less truthful—that is to say, they more or less correctly reflect reality and correspond with it.

But this is not the only way in which ideas are formed. They are also formed in a more indirect and roundabout way. And ideas formed in a more indirect and roundabout way are profoundly influential in the formation of ideologies.

This roundabout process which enters into the formation of ideologies involves three main steps. First, abstract ideas are formed on the basis of various social relationships and experiences of people. Second, those abstract ideas are separated from the actual experiences and relationships from which they were derived. Third, both particular conclusions and general ideas about all kinds of things are then worked out with the aid of those abstract ideas.

For example, when society divides into classes and a ruling class is formed, then, on the basis of definite social relations and social experiences and activities, there is formed the abstract idea of the relationship between ruler and ruled and of the power and prerogatives of the ruler. From that, the next step is to separate this abstract idea from the actual experiences and relationships from which it was originally derived, to consider it as expressing a general truth about the universe, and to go on to form the idea of God, the ruler of the universe. The third and last step is to proceed to interpret existing social relations as decreed by God, and to interpret nature as the creation of God.

When ideas about things are formed and worked out in this way, it means that we are approaching things with certain more or less fixed preconceptions about them already in our minds. Indeed, such preconceptions are often so fixed in our minds as a result of education and habit, that we never dream of questioning them, but take them as axioms, as natural and obvious ways of thinking. And then we form our general views and particular conclusions about things not primarily as a result of critical investigation and practical verification of conclusions but independent of practice, uncritically, without investigation.

When ideas about things are formed in this way, then they generally cease to be truthful and become more or less illusory. They do not correctly reflect and correspond with reality, but, on the contrary, they give an incorrect, illusory, fantastic or distorted picture of reality.

Illusions, however, are always founded in reality. They are

not pure inventions of the mind, but they arise, as we have just seen, by a process of forming ideas from one source, and then generalising them and using them as preconceptions applied in many different contexts, replacing the critical formation and verification of ideas through actual practice and experience.

Every illusion has its source in reality. It reflects definite conditions of material life, arises from definite social relations, experiences and activities. That is why many illusions are so persistent. It is not simply a question of the indoctrination of individuals with certain illusory ideas, but it is a question of existing social relations continually generating certain illusions, and of these illusions serving definite material interests.

Illusions take two main forms.

In the first place, there arise illusions about real things—misconceptions of real processes and relations familiar in experience and practice. Such, for example, is the illusion that certain social relations and institutions follow from human nature, or were decreed by Reason.

In the second place, illusions develop into sheer mythology and fantasy, the invention of imaginary things. Thus people not only misconceive nature and society, both of which really exist, but they also form ideas of heaven and hell, of the spiritual world, and so on, which have no existence; they invent all kinds of imaginary beings, such as gods, fairies and devils.

In this connection, we should note that illusion cannot be simply equated with error. Of course, illusion is error; but it is a special kind of error.

Suppose, for example, that someone says that thirteen squared equals 166. This is a simple error, an error in calculation (since the right answer is 169). But suppose, on the other hand, he says that thirteen is an unlucky number. This is not like an error in calculation, which can be made by people possessing on the whole correct ideas about numbers. It expresses an illusion, namely, the illusion that numbers are lucky or unlucky. Such an error does not arise simply from a mistake in operating with numbers, but it arises from applying to numbers preconceived ideas about luck which, though they have a definite source in experience and practice, are wrongly and uncritically applied to numbers.

Similarly, if someone says that the British Constitution was introduced into Parliament by Oliver Cromwell, this is an erroneous statement, arising from an insufficient study of British constitutional history. But suppose he says that the British Constitution is an expression of the unique genius of the Anglo-Saxon race, or is God's gift to the British people. These statements, though also erroneous, are not simply errors in history. They arise from applying to social affairs preconceived ideas about racial genius or God.

Thus illusions constitute a special kind of error, arising from a quite definite mode of misconceiving things in terms of preconceived ideas.

Scientific and Illusory Ideology

Both processes of the formation of abstract ideas—that is to say, both the process of forming more or less truthful ideas critically through practical experience and interaction with things, and the process of forming more or less illusory ideas as preconceptions applied in the formation of views—enter into the formation of actual ideologies. At the same time, one or other of these processes may dominate in the constitution of particular ideologies, so that they are predominantly scientific in the one case or predominantly illusory and unscientific in the other case.

All ideology in class-divided society is developed by the intellectual representatives of definite classes, and corresponds to the actual position and serves the requirements of definite classes in their class struggle. This being so, we can see how inevitably the two processes interact and interpenetrate in the formation of class ideologies.

On the one hand, in so far as the interests of a class do demand a true apprehension of reality based on critical investigation of some kind, its ideology does contain a scientific element. For example, the class interests of the capitalist class certainly do require that considerable work should be done on discovering the real laws governing various natural processes, and such discoveries do play their part in bourgeois ideology. The same interests also require that certain social investigations should be carried on, and from this source again a certain scientific element does enter into bourgeois ideology.

On the other hand, in so far as the interests of a class and the place it occupies in social production give rise to certain preconceptions and illusions which serve the class in its struggle, its ideology is illusory. And so, for example, if we consider bourgeois ideology, there are many elements in it which merely embody the illusions of the bourgeois class and the views peculiar to bourgeois society.

Bourgeois ideology, indeed, is formed by the development of both processes. And this gives rise to contradictions in its development, since the products of the two processes continually come into contradiction and the resolution of such contradictions has to be sought in the development of ideology. The same has been true of the ideologies of other classes, though the scientific element is far stronger in bourgeois ideology, so that the contradictions have become sharper.

Thus in the development of bourgeois philosophy, for example, there has been a continual effort to reconcile scientific discoveries with bourgeois preconceptions. The most obvious way in which this contradiction has expressed itself in bourgeois philosophy is in the contradiction between the materialist picture of the world afforded by scientific discoveries and the religious views which form an essential part of the ideological preconceptions. Philosophers have continually sought ways and means of resolving this contradiction ; they keep resolving it to their own satisfaction, and as often as they resolve it, it crops up again.

Again, in bourgeois science, discoveries are always being interpreted—with the help of philosophers—in terms of the bourgeois preconceptions. We can see this happening today, for example, in the development of physics, where the discoveries of quantum physics are interpreted as meaning that events are unpredictable and their real nature unknowable. This is simply an application in physical science of bourgeois ideological preconceptions generated by the general crisis of capitalism. On the other hand, certain preconceptions, at least in their old forms, have had to be given up and replaced by others, because of their contradiction with advancing knowledge of nature. This has happened, for example, with religious doctrines, which have often been modified in the course of the struggle to reconcile religion with science—as when the theologians eventually ditched both Adam and Eve as a concession to the theory of evolution.

Considering such examples, we can see that the opposition and interpenetration of scientific and illusory elements in ideology cannot be conceived so simply, as if ideas about one thing were scientific while ideas about some other thing were illusory. The fact is rather that scientific and illusory elements oppose each other and interpenetrate in the ideas formed about one and the same thing.

Thus bourgeois ideology, for example, is a contradictory compound of truthful and illusory elements, with the latter always persisting and maintaining themselves. It might be said that the scientific element is stronger in the bourgeois views about natural processes, while the illusory element is stronger in the bourgeois views about social processes. But both elements enter into all parts and all fields of bourgeois ideology, and the illusory element is the most characteristic feature of the ideology. What stamps bourgeois ideology as peculiarly bourgeois is the character of its illusions.

The same may be said of other ideologies of the past. At the same time, we may consistently claim, and do claim, that Socialist or Marxist ideology is primarily a scientific ideology, and in this respect distinguishes itself from every other ideology without exception. This is because the struggle to end capitalism and, with it, all exploitation of man by man, which this ideology serves, does demand above all a true apprehension of reality and opposes itself to all the illusions of societies based on exploitation.

CHAPTER SEVEN

IDEOLOGICAL ILLUSIONS

Ideological illusions have their source in the production relations of society. But they are not consciously derived from that source, but arise unconsciously or spontaneously. Unaware of the true source of their illusory ideas, ideologists imagine they have produced them by a process of pure thought. And so there takes place a process of inversion in ideology, by which real social relations are represented as the realisation of abstract ideas. Lastly, ideological illusions constitute a class-motivated system of deception.

Ideological Reflection of Production Relations

IN this chapter we shall consider the development of ideological preconceptions or illusions, and will then turn, in the next two chapters, to the development of scientific ideas.

There are five main, characteristic features of the development of ideological illusions in class-divided society, which can be traced in every ideology up to and including bourgeois ideology.

(1) The first feature of ideological illusions is that they always arise as reflections of particular, historically constituted relations of production. Their source is the production relations of society.

In the development of ideological illusions, it seems as if abstract ideas, general theories, were being spun out of people's heads—developed and controlled, to all appearances, simply by the thinking process itself. Yet how did such ideas come into people's heads ? What is their source ? Unless we are to believe that ideas are formed spontaneously in the mind, or that we are born already equipped with " innate ideas ", then we must suppose that a source in objective reality outside the mind can be found for all our ideas, including the most abstract and illusory—a source from which they are derived and of which they are the reflection.

Consciousness is never anything but a reflection of material existence. First there is matter, objective being, and then, secondarily, there is consciousness, the reflection of matter. The mind has no inner sources of its own, from which ideas can be derived. Every idea, every element of ideology, is derived from and reflects some objective reality, some real aspect of the material world.

The source of the illusions in ideology is always the real economic structure of society. As men live, so do they think. Corresponding to the relations they enter into in producing the means of life, they produce social ideas and social theories.

Thus, for example, it is the real relations of landowners and serfs established in the feudal mode of production that are reflected in the feudal ideas of landownership, and in feudal ideology in general. Similarly, it is the capitalist relationships which are reflected in capitalist ideology. And it was the far simpler relationships within the tribe, the solidarity of the individual with the tribe, which were reflected in the " primitive " ideology of primitive communism.

Thus as society develops, the ideas which reflect the property relations of society become elaborated in the form of systems and theories concerning politics, social rights and obligations, law, and so on. All such ideology has its source in the social relations of production, and constitutes, in the last analysis, nothing but an ideological reflection of those relations.

The same is true of moral ideas. If we have ideas of absolute standards of good and bad, right and wrong, virtue and vice, these ideas are reflections not of any objective property of persons or actions but of the social relations into which people have entered and within which their personal activity takes place. No wonder, therefore, that moral judgments change with fundamental changes in social relations ; and that there is only one objective standard for saying that one morality is higher than another, namely, that it reflects and serves a higher social system.

And the same is true of the ideology of the supernatural, of religious ideology. The supernatural world which men conjure up for themselves in their ideas is never, in the last analysis, anything other than a reflection of the real world of society, of the social relations within which men live their earthly lives. The world of the supernatural always serves as the guardian of the basic fabric of society. The tribal religion stands guard over the tribe and protects tribal relations, just as the ideas of Christianity today have been so adapted that heaven seems to stand guard over the bourgeois order of society. The supernatural world which guards and justifies the social order is created in the image of that social order.

These are examples of the way in which various forms of ideological illusions are developed in terms of abstract ideas whose source lies in the development of social relations, more precisely, of the relations of production. The objective reality which is reflected in such ideas is never anything else than the existing complex of social relations which spring from the production of the material means of life.

The Spontaneous Character of Ideological Illusion

(2) The second feature of ideological illusions is that, although their source lies in the complex of real social relations, they are neither consciously derived from that source nor are they put forward as an analysis of existing social relations.

The ideas which people employ may reflect their social relations, but their ideological illusions are not created by their *consciously* reflecting on their own social relations and working out for themselves, in a scientific manner, an accurate and systematic account of the social structure which they find in existence.

The ideas of political economy, for example, as set forth in such a book as Marx's *Capital*, are derived from a conscious, methodical investigation of actually existing relations of production. Precisely for that reason they are not illusory but scientific in character. Ideological illusion, on the other hand, arises precisely as an unconscious, unintended reflection of an existing social structure, expressed in general ideas about the world. It has an unconscious, spontaneous character. That is why, if we want to discover the most essential features of some illusory ideology, we shall not discover them in the reasoned forms in which men have presented their ideas, but rather in the unreasoned assumptions, the preconceptions which they take for granted, which underly their reasoning.

For example, in the ideology of the medieval Catholic Church, the whole world, heaven and earth, was regarded as a hierarchy in which the lower members were necessarily subordinate to the higher. In the production of this ideology there was no intention of giving an account of the feudal order ; the conscious intention was to give an account of the necessary order of the whole world, and this was consciously worked out as a logical system. But yet the ideology was in fact a reflection of the existing feudal social relations, which were thus reproduced in men's ideas by a spontaneous, unintended, unconscious process. The general ideas employed were a reflection of actual social relations, but they were not consciously produced as such a reflection, but arose unconsciously and spontaneously in men's minds. These ideas then became fixed as preconceptions which were used for the purpose of interpreting and working out the theory of everything which people were interested in, whether in nature or society or the imaginary realm of heaven.

The spontaneous, unconscious character of the ideological reflection of relations of production is due to the spontaneous, unconscious character of those relations of production themselves.

Men's relations of production, wrote Marx, are " indispensable and independent of their will". This is the key to understanding the nature of the illusory ideological reflection of those relations in abstract ideas about the world and society. The given relations of production are not deliberately instituted, but they are at the same time, at the given stage of social development, indispensable. And because people never decided to institute them but at the same time cannot get on without them, they are not conscious of them as transitory social relations which have been instituted at a definite time, in definite circumstances, to answer definite but only temporary historical needs of society. Rather do they appear as part of the necessary order of things. The characteristic features of men's social relations and relationships with nature, which are in fact the historically determined result of a definite mode of production, are reflected in abstract ideas in the form of preconceptions and illusions about the nature of man and society, as ideas about God and divine providence, about right and justice, about the eternal and necessary characteristics of all being, the ultimate nature of reality, and so on.

The Illusion of Pure Thought

(3) The third feature of ideological illusions is that, just because their spontaneous character precludes people's being aware of their true source, they seem to themselves to have produced them by a free process of thought, by a pure and unfettered operation of the mind.

" Ideology[1] is a process accomplished by the so-called thinker consciously, indeed, but with a false consciousness," wrote Engels. " The real motives impelling him remain unknown to him, otherwise it would not be an ideological process at all. Hence he imagines false or apparent motives. Because it is a process of thought, he derives both its form and its content

---

[1] Marx and Engels frequently used the term " ideology " to refer exclusively to the process of ideological illusion, thus employing it in a restricted sense. When the term is used in this restricted sense, then scientific modes of thought are by definition excluded from the ideological process, and such an expression as " scientific ideology " becomes a contradiction in terms, like, say, " round square ". Lenin and Stalin, on the other hand, often used the term " ideology " in a wider sense, so that they speak, for example, of " scientific socialist ideology ", and characterise Marxism as such an ideology.

In this book I have employed the term throughout in the wider sense, so that the word " ideology " is used to denote the typical outlook or theory of a period or of a class, in which both illusory and truthful or scientific elements may enter, and which, with the rise of the revolutionary working class movement and of socialism, becomes primarily scientific and dispenses with the illusory modes of thought of previous ideologies.

from pure thought, either his own or that of his predecessors. He works with mere thought material which he accepts without examination as the product of thought, and he does not investigate further for a more remote process independent of thought."[1]

And again, Engels wrote that ideology—the working out of ideological illusions—is "occupation with thoughts as with independent entities, developing independently and subject only to their own laws. That the material life conditions of the persons inside whose heads this thought process goes on in the last resort determine the course of this process, remains of necessity unknown to these persons, for otherwise there would be an end of all ideology."[2]

Ideological Inversion

(4) The fourth feature of ideological illusions is that a process of inversion takes place in them, by which real social relations are represented as the realisation of abstract ideas.

In the process of ideological illusion, products of abstract thought are treated as though they were independent of the material social relations which they in fact reflect. And so it follows that reality is turned upside down in this process. The source of abstract ideas is taken to be the mind, rather than the material reality of social relations. And so the ultimate ground for the existence of those relations themselves is conceived as being the abstractions of the mind.

According to this inverted way of looking at things, men create their social relationships in obedience to their abstract ideas, and not the other way round.

Take, for example, abstract conceptions of right and justice, which constitute an important part of all ideology. Abstract right and justice are represented as independent of actual social relationships, and those relationships are represented as reflecting and realising—perhaps imperfectly—an abstract right and justice. According to this topsy-turvy way of looking at things,

[1] Engels, *Letter* to Mehring, July 14, 1893.
[2] Engels, *Ludwig Feuerbach*, ch. 4.

the abstract ideas of right and justice seem to determine the real relationships of men, whereas in fact it is the real relationships of men that determine their ideas of right and justice. And similarly, the social system seems to be justified by how far it corresponds to abstract ideas of right and justice, whereas in fact ideas of right and justice are justified by how far they serve the material progress of society.

" Economic, political and other reflections are just like those in the human eye," wrote Engels. " They pass through a condensing lens and therefore appear upside down, standing on their heads. Only the nervous system which would put them on their feet again for representation is lacking. . . . This inversion . . . forms what we call ideological conception."[1]

And Marx and Engels further wrote :

" If in all ideology men and their circumstances appear upside down as in a camera obscura, this phenomenon arises just as much from their historical life process as the inversion of objects on the retina does from their physical life process."[2]

As a result of this ideological inversion, it follows that in every epoch people have shared the illusion that their institutions and public activities are the expression of their abstract ideas—of their religion, philosophy, political principles, and so on. Thus the slave owners of ancient Rome thought of themselves as actuated by republican principles, just as modern capitalists thought of themselves (and still try to get others to think of them) as actuated by democratic principles. The wars of the Middle Ages were fought avowedly for religious principles, just as the wars of today are fought avowedly for national or political principles.

[1] Engels, *Letter* to C. Schmidt, October 27, 1890.

[2] Marx and Engels, *The German Ideology*, Part I, ch. 1. They are referring to the fact that the image formed on the lens of a camera or on the retina of the eye is always upside down. In the case of the eye, this inversion is corrected in the visual parts of the brain, so that we finally become visually conscious of things the right way up—just as a similar correction is made in the process of photography.

According to this way of looking at things, wrote Marx, " each principle has had its own century in which to manifest itself. The principle of authority, for example, had the eleventh century, just as the principle of individualism had the eighteenth century . . . it was the century that belonged to the principle, and not the principle to the century. In other words, it was the principle that made the history, and not the history that made the principle".[1]

Every epoch, then, produces its characteristic illusions, which are expressed in its dominant ideology—illusions as to the real grounds and motive forces of its institutions and activities.

" For instance," wrote Marx and Engels, " . . . an epoch imagines itself to be actuated by purely political or religious motives, although religion and politics are only forms of its true motives . . ." It is this which constitutes " the illusion of that epoch ". In this illusion, " the idea, the conception of these conditioned men about their real practice is transformed into the sole determining active force which controls and determines their practice".[2]

In ideological illusion, the products of the mind are represented as the dominating, compelling influence in human affairs. And so it also happens that these products of the mind, which are mere distorted fantasms of real conditions of existence, come to be endowed in men's imaginations with a real existence of their own. In this way are created what Marx called " the mist-enveloped regions of the religious world. In that world the productions of the human brain appear as independent beings endowed with life, and entering into relation both with one another and the human race".[3]

And so, while men imagine their whole social life and institutions to be based on and motivated by their ideology, at the same time this ideology conjures up a fantastic world of powers and forces superior to and independent of both man and nature, to which men feel themselves subject, on

[1] Marx, *The Poverty of Philosophy*, ch. 2, section 1, 5th observation.
[2] Marx and Engels, *The German Ideology*, Part I, ch. 1.
[3] Marx, *Capital*, Vol. I, ch. 1, section 4.

which their destinies seem to depend and whose aid they seek
to enlist for their enterprises.

The " religious world ", as Marx said, is never anything " but
the reflection of the real world ".[1]

In the most primitive social organisations men are relatively
helpless in the face of natural forces ; they are banded together
to get a living, and would be doomed to destruction without
this elementary social cohesion and co-operation. This fact is
reflected in their minds in the illusions of magic. Men seem
to possess a special power and virtue as members of their tribe
or clan, and this virtue takes the form, in their imagination,
of a special magical force. All sorts of procedures are invented
for exerting it—and later, with division of labour, it comes
to be regarded as the possession and concern of certain individuals only, and not of the whole people. At the same time,
natural objects and natural forces are assumed to be animated,
and are later personified ; so that the whole intercourse of
man with man, and of man with nature, is represented as
depending on the activity of unseen, mysterious powers.

The development and ramification of religious ideas has
kept pace with and reflected the development of men's social
life.

" The primitive religious notions, which in the main are
common to each group of kindred peoples," wrote Engels,
" develop, after the separation of the group, in a manner peculiar
to each people, according to the living conditions falling to
their lot."[2]

As with all ideology, religion is not created anew in each new
phase of social development. On the contrary, every ideology
in its development makes use of traditional materials which
are taken over from previous ideology, and incorporates in
itself materials borrowed from other ideologies. It is the same
in religion ; and so, for example, we can still recognise even
in the religious doctrines and practices of Protestant Christianity
today elements which have been carried over from primitive

[1] *Ibid.*
[2] Engels, *Ludwig Feuerbach*, ch. 4.

tribal magic, overlaid and transformed as they may be with new meanings.

"Religion, once formed," wrote Engels, "always contains traditional material, just as in all ideological domains tradition is a great conservative force. But the transformations which this material undergoes spring from class relations—that is to say, out of the economic relations of the persons who execute these transformations."[1]

This characteristic of all ideological illusion—that, because it is occupation with thoughts as with independent entities, it continually develops ideas out of the material of other ideas—effectively disguises the fact that every ideology, and every element of ideology, is but a reflection of material social existence, and makes it appear as though it were really what it purports to be, an independent march of ideas.

The nature of ideology is never obvious on the surface, but comes to light only as a result of Marx's profound scientific discovery, that "the mode of production of material life conditions the social, political and intellectual life process in general ".[2]

So long as men are not the masters of their own social organisation, so long are their real social relations reflected in ideological inversions which, far from rendering their real social relations intelligible, mystify them and conceal their real character, together with the real springs and laws of human social action, behind a veil of religious, political, legal, artistic and philosophical illusions.

Ideology and Class Interest

(5) The fifth feature of ideological illusions is that, in society divided into classes, they constitute a class-motivated system of deception, a mode of disguising the real social relations in the interests of a definite class.

Illusion always reflects the real social relations in such a way as to disguise them.

[1] *Ibid.*
[2] Marx, *Critique of Political Economy*, Preface.

For example, the religious ideology of the Middle Ages, with its conception of a heavenly hierarchy which reflected the feudal order, meant that the exploitation of the serf by the lord was disguised as a subordination cf the serf to his natural superiors under the rule of God. And similarly, the naked fact that the feudal lord appropriated the produce of the serf's labour was disguised by the abstract feudal ideas of ownership, dues, rights and obligations.

Once again, the naked fact that the capitalist appropriates the values produced by the workers' unpaid labour is disguised by the abstract capitalist ideas of ownership, contract and equality of rights. This disguise is completed by capitalist forms of religion. That is why, though bourgeois ideology has often taken non-religious or anti-religious forms, it always leaves a loophole for religion and continually comes back to it, while in periods of crisis, when the system is seriously endangered, religious ideology is always brought to the fore and takes the offensive.

" For a society based upon the production of commodities," wrote Marx, " in which the producers in general enter into social relations with one another by treating their products as commodities and values, whereby they reduce their individual private labour to the standard of homogeneous human labour—for such a society, Christianity, with its cultus of abstract man, more especially in its bourgeois developments, Protestantism, Deism, etc., is the most fitting form of religion."[1]

The whole of bourgeois ideology, from its religion to its political economy, disguises the fact of capitalist exploitation.

The disguise and deception inherent in all ideological illusion is always socially motivated. In other words, it serves definite social ends, definite social interests.

In primitive societies, before the birth of classes, it serves to strengthen and consolidate the bonds of solidarity between members of the tribe, on which their survival depends. And in conditions when people are almost totally ignorant of the natural forces which environ them, magical ideas make them

[1] Marx, *Capital*, Vol. I, ch. 1, section 4.

feel that nevertheless they can control these forces. Primitive ideology is thus motivated by the self-preservation of the whole tribe, by the interest of the whole people to preserve their social organisation and to feel strong and secure in it.

When society splits into antagonistic classes, and when, consequently, history becomes the history of class struggles, then class interest becomes the main motivation of ideology. Every ideology becomes the ideology of a class, expressing, in however roundabout a way, the conditions of existence of a definite class and serving that class in its struggle against other classes. The dominant ideology in any period is that of the ruling class. And when this ideology is challenged, that is but the expression of the fact that the existing state of class relations is being challenged by another class.

The disguise and deception of class ideology, motivated as it is by class interest, is not to be interpreted, however, as primarily a deliberate, conscious deception.

To suppose that the thinking representatives of a class deliberately invent misleading ideas with the conscious purpose of disguising from the people what they know to be the real character of the social relations is to suppose that these thinkers do in fact know what is the real character of the social relations. But the very essence of ideological illusion is that it is a false consciousness of social relations. The mystifying ideological conception of these relations takes the place of a correct, scientific conception. This false consciousness arises, as we have seen, not by a deliberate process but rather by a spontaneous, unconscious process. It is not deliberate falsehood but—illusion. If it is deception, it is also self-deception.

Those who would interpret ideological illusions as mere deliberate deceptions, therefore, mistake the very nature of what Marx and Engels called " false consciousness ". For they suppose that the class whose interests are served by the ideology possesses in fact a true consciousness of the basis of its existence—which is just what no exploiting class possesses or ever can possess. The explanation of ideologies as products of well-laid plans to deceive the people in the interests of a class is an absurd vulgarisation of Marxism. That is not how ideologies arise.

Of course, spokesmen and ideologists of ruling classes do constantly engage in conscious, deliberate deception of the people. But behind the system of deliberate deception lies always a system of self-deception.

As a case in point we may take the example of Plato, who was a representative of extreme ideological reaction in ancient Greece. He advocated that, to keep the people down, the rulers should propagate what he called " a noble lie " : although they knew very well it was not true, they should proclaim that rulers and ruled were men of two different kinds, the rulers being " golden " men and the rest being men of mere " brass and iron ".[1] At the same time, Plato maintained that aristocracy was the best system of society and that any departure from it meant anarchy and degeneration. This, however, he undoubtedly believed. It was one of the illusions of his class, and constituted the very basis of his outlook. From the point of view of the aristocratic slave-owners' ideology, which Plato expounded and which he did much to shape, it was quite in order to tell the people lies, and such lies were " noble ".

Such has been the situation with all ruling class ideologies. Genuine false consciousness becomes involved in deliberate deception, so that the two become closely intertwined and even, at times, indistinguishable. This is especially the case in capitalist society, in which all things, including ideas, are bought and sold. Those who have ideas to sell come to regard them as commodities to be exchanged for cash, not as truths to be believed.

The class-motivated character of particular ideologies has long been recognised. When a new class is rising to power, and consequently posing a new ideology against that of the old ruling class, it generally recognises that the old ideology expresses the interests of its political opponents. It attacks this ideology, therefore, as a system of falsehoods motivated by class interest. It advances its own ideology, on the other

[1] Plato, *Republic*, Book III.

hand, as a system of truth, corresponding to the profounder needs of the whole of society.

" Each new class which puts itself in the place of the one ruling before it", wrote Marx and Engels, " is compelled, merely in order to carry through its aim, to represent its interest as the common interest of all the members of society, put in an ideal form ; it will give its ideas the form of universality, and represent them as the only rational, universally valid ones. The class making a revolution appears from the very start, merely because it is opposed to a *class*, not as a class, but as the representative of the whole of society."[1]

A newly formed ideology, therefore, generally starts with a profound impulse to development, as a universal system of ideas opening up new horizons, corresponding to deeply felt social needs, as if it were based not on the interests of a class but on the aspirations of a whole people. In the course of time, however, as the new ruling and exploiting class becomes entangled in its own contradictions, its ideology loses its revolutionary elan and becomes conservative ; it begins to decay and disintegrate ; until finally it stands revealed in its turn as a system of class-motivated deceptions, while its exponents degenerate from original thinkers into mere hired propagandists of the ruling class.

[1] Marx and Engels, *The German Ideology*, Part I, ch. 1.

CHAPTER EIGHT

SCIENCE

In contrast to ideological illusion, people discover truth in the course of their practical activity. The first source of such discovery lies in social production. From the ideas derived in the productive process arise natural sciences, which take the form of specialised investigations separated from production and carried on by particular classes, who introduce elements of their class ideology into the sciences. At the same time, social sciences are developed, with their roots in experiences gained in class struggle, serving the ends of the general management and control of social affairs. But in the hands of exploiting classes the social sciences can never attain the scientific status of the natural sciences.

The Ideas of the Production Process

ALONG with the development of the illusory, inverted reflection in consciousness of the relations of production goes the development of men's true ideas of the material objects which environ them with which they are concerned in the process of production, of the production process itself and of their own activities and social relations.

For the development of production, and of the social intercourse which arises from production, demands and gives rise to the working out of true ideas about things and their interconnections and motions, and about various human activities and relations. Unless people do obtain such true ideas, they cannot successfully carry on production or manage their social affairs. And the more various and powerful their forces of production, and the more various and complex their social activities, the more do they need to find out about nature and about themselves in order to bring their various projects to a successful conclusion.

In the development of abstract ideology, as Marx and Engels

pointed out, " consciousness can really flatter itself that it is something other than consciousness of existing practice". But at the same time as consciousness thus abstracts itself from existing practice, the consciousness of existing practice also develops as practice develops. That very development of production, of division of labour, and of relations of production, which leads to illusory flights of inverted ideology, also leads to a growth of men's true ideas about their real conditions of life.

Such true ideas do not arise of themselves. They have to be laboriously formed, worked out and tested in practice. They represent so many *discoveries* made by people in the course of their social practice.

The first source of people's discoveries is the practice of social production.

We have already seen that it is a characteristic of the social process of production that in it men have an idea of what they aim to produce. There is and can be no production, in the human sense, not even the most primitive kinds of food-gathering and hunting, without this consciousness. And so in producing, men are also necessarily forming their ideas of the objects with which they come into relation, of the materials they use and the techniques which they employ, and making discoveries about the properties of those objects and materials and about what can be done with them.

" The elementary factors of the labour process ", wrote Marx, " are (1) the personal activity of man, i.e., work itself, (2) the subject of work, and (3) its instruments."[1] And none of these factors can be set in motion without corresponding ideas and discoveries. With development of production and division of labour, the forms of work become more varied, its subject extends and its instruments are improved. And this means that men's ideas are correspondingly enlarged and that they make new discoveries.

Primitive man, for example, who expressed his social relations and relationships with nature in a magical ideology, had already

[1] Marx, *Capital*, Vol. I, ch. 7, section 1.

very precise and accurate ideas of the different species of animals which he hunted, and of their various habits and properties—as is shown, among other things, by the records he made of his knowledge in cave paintings.[1] With the development of agriculture and handicrafts new discoveries were made and men's ideas of natural objects and their properties, and of the principles involved in the various production processes, were greatly enlarged. And now, in modern capitalist society, the very same institutes and universities which churn out all manner of bourgeois religious, political and philosophical illusions, are the repositories of a vast and growing store of accurate and systematic knowledge of nature and of the principles by the application of which man advances his mastery of nature; all this is the fruit of thousands of years of human endeavour and, in particular, of the mighty advances in production achieved in the capitalist era.

Thus if men's illusions have their ultimate source in the relations of production, men also continually make discoveries which arise in the last analysis from the production process itself. In these discoveries there is a development of abstract ideas which reflect various features and properties of things and of the production process without ideological preconception, inversion or disguise.

Such ideas of nature and of technological processes constitute, in fact, an important aspect of the productive forces themselves. The forces of production include people, with their production experience and skill. People's production experience and skill is recorded, generalised and systematised in their ideas; and, equipped with these ideas, they utilise the instruments of production and also improve them. Further, the growth of knowledge of the production process, of its subjects and instruments, of the principles of technology and of nature generally, is not only an essential condition for the continuance of production at a given level; under suitable conditions it contributes to new advances of production, and

---

[1] I am indebted for this observation to Dr. Donald Ross, who is working on a history of the biological sciences.

so may become one of the factors making eventually necessary revolutionary changes in the relations of production to bring them into correspondence with new forces of production.

The Rise of Natural Sciences

The natural sciences spring from the ideas, or the knowledge, accumulated in the production process.

" From the very beginning", Engels wrote, " the origin and development of the sciences has been determined by production."[1]

Throughout antiquity, he observed, scientific investigation proper remained restricted to astronomy, mathematics and mechanics. For " astronomy . . . if only on account of the seasons, was absolutely indispensable for pastoral and agricultural peoples. Astronomy can only develop with the aid of mathematics. Hence this also had to be tackled. Further, at a certain stage of agriculture and in certain regions (raising of water for irrigation in Egypt), and especially with the origin of towns, big building operations and the development of handicrafts—mechanics. This was soon needed also for navigation and war. Moreover, it requires the aid of mathematics and so promotes the latter's development." Later, with the great new developments of the forces of production which led to and then took place within the capitalist system, new sciences arose one after the other—physics, chemistry, the biological sciences, geology. " If . . . the sciences suddenly arose anew with undreamed-of force, developing at a miraculous rate, once again we owe this miracle to—production."[2]

If the development of the sciences is determined by production, this also accounts for the uneven rate in history of the development of the sciences and for the often one-sided character of that development. The varying character of production and of the emphasis placed on different production processes accounts for it. Thus chemistry, for example, was never far developed until modern times, though mechanics and certain parts of the biological sciences had a considerable

[1] Engels, *Dialectics of Nature*, Notes.
[2] *Ibid.*

development. Again, the agricultural sciences are relatively neglected under modern monopoly capitalism, while all the sciences connected with war production are energetically fostered.

Sciences as Specialised Undertakings Distinct from Production

Sciences are essentially specialised undertakings, with their own specialist techniques and theories. The rise of sciences occurs when, as a product of division of labour, there begins a special investigation of the properties of various natural objects and natural processes, distinct from production itself; and when, consequently, there also occurs a special elaboration, a generalisation and systematisation, of ideas in connection with such investigation.

Only under such conditions may we speak of sciences. Thus we would hardly allow the title of " science " to the knowledge possessed by primitive tribes, extensive and accurate as it is, of the various kinds of animals and plants, or of the properties of various materials, or of the succession of the seasons. Such knowledge is raised to the level of science only when these things are made the subjects of special investigation distinct from actual production—in the first place from hunting, making tools, gardening and the like; and when, consequently, what is discovered about them is generalised and systematised as a special body of knowledge.

We may distinguish three outstanding characteristics of sciences, which progressively distinguish scientific theory from the knowledge of natural objects and processes inherent in the production process itself and constituting the producers' own consciousness of their work, its subjects and instruments.

(1) Sciences engage in *systematic description and classification* of natural objects and processes. Such, for example, is the charting of the heavenly bodies and their apparent movements undertaken by the pioneers of astronomical science, like the ancient Egyptians; or the " natural histories " compiled by early students of living nature, like Aristotle, whose zoological works comprised a systematic description and classification of most known (as well as some imaginary) kinds of animals with

attempts at formulating laws correlating the various properties of different animals.

(2) Basing themselves on such description and classification of natural objects and their motions, sciences proceed by abstraction to formulate the *principles and laws* manifested in and governing the observed properties and motions of natural objects. By such abstraction, for example, are derived such concepts as mass, momentum, etc., in mechanics ; or the concepts of number and geometrical form in mathematics.

(3) Utilising such concepts, the sciences proceed by the formulation of *hypotheses*. Such hypotheses seek to *explain* the observed properties, interconnections and motions of the things investigated, and so to *predict* their further properties, interconnections and motions ; they seek to provide a systematic theory of the phenomena, and to enable men to understand and make use of them.

Consequently, while science has its roots in production, and is applied in production, at the same time it is developed as a specialised activity distinct from production.

It follows that those who develop it are frequently unaware of, and may even deny, its connection with production. So far as their own consciousness of their activities is concerned, they may be carrying out their investigations out of curiosity, sheerly for the sake of knowledge, from love of mankind and the desire to enlighten people, because they enjoy it, because they are paid to do it, because they wish to become famous, or because they wish to do opponents a bad turn by proving them wrong. Many different subjective motives may and do operate in scientific work, and, of course, these motives may and do influence the character and outcome of the work.

Further, once science is put on the track of certain discoveries, these often lead of themselves to others, and the process of following up conclusions and generalising and systematising the resulting ideas proceeds with a logic of its own, independent of particular practical problems connected with production.

For this reason important scientific problems are often elucidated in advance of practical needs and even long before any practical application is possible. For example, scientific conclusions about the existence of electromagnetic waves were reached well in advance of any practical application in radio techniques. Atomic fission was discovered many years before any practical application of the release of atomic energy was attempted. Thus scientific advance tends to acquire a momentum of its own independent of practical application. What is more, even when that application becomes technically possible, it is often delayed on account of political and economic circumstances.[1]

Sciences, as the theory of production, are thus from the outset distinct from the practice of production, both in their organisation and in the personal activity and consciousness of their practitioners. At the same time, the character of the sciences and their level do always depend on those of production, their problems arise in the last analysis from production, and their results are fed back into production. The development of sciences is always dependent on the development of production, and in turn sustains and pushes forward production. The distinction of science from production is not a disconnection, but a very close connection. And in proportion as this underlying connection ever becomes severed, the sciences themselves always begin to stagnate and then to decay. In general, the times when a new impetus is given to science are times when new techniques of production are being developed. Those who then pioneer the new paths in science are usually closely associated in their practical interests with the new productive processes. Then follows a process of the scientific elaboration and development of the new ideas and discoveries. But this process cannot be long sustained if it fails to achieve technical application and lacks the stimulus of problems arising from that application.

---

[1] See J. D. Bernal, *Science and Industry in the Nineteenth Century*. London, 1953.

Science and Classes

What has been said shows that the rise of sciences is a product of division of labour. Sciences are developed as a product of mental as distinct from physical labour—as a special field of theoretical activity separated from the labour of production. It follows from this that the development of the sciences is closely bound up with that of classes. At different times different classes have taken a hand in the development of the sciences and have, in consequence, influenced that development to suit their class requirements, and imposed on the sciences certain features of their class ideology.

From the division of labour arose private property and exploiting classes, and so the division between the mass of producers, wholly engaged in productive toil, and the privileged and leisured minority who took over the general management and direction of society. The development of sciences, as a branch of mental labour, was dependent upon the existence of such a minority, freed from the physical labour of production and able to undertake such mental labour.

Thus the class which, in any particular period, has taken over the general management and direction of society, and therefore of the state, religion and so on, also takes charge of the sciences and exercises a controlling influence over their development.

Sciences develop essentially as part of the means which are required for the general direction and management of social affairs, as well as of particular undertakings. Hence the sciences develop as means or instruments in the hands of various classes, serving their requirements in the way of (a) carrying on and expanding production, and (b) managing and controlling social affairs generally. These classes promote and foster the development of sciences in so far as their interests require that they find things out, as distinct from merely remaining in ignorance or inventing false theories.

Thus the expansion of science, and also the limits to that expansion, are governed by the interests arising from the conditions of existence of particular classes from time to time.

In slave society and in feudal society, for example, the conditions of existence of the ruling classes, which were bound up with the existence of a comparatively low level of development of both agriculture and industry, dictated only a most limited interest in the development of sciences. But once the bourgeoisie arose, its interests demanded an enormous extension of scientific work, connected primarily with the development of manufactures and industries, but also, in the conditions of its revolutionary struggle, with man and his social relations. Modern science is the creation of the bourgeoisie, one of the most typical products of bourgeois society, the means for understanding and controlling the processes of nature and society created under the conditions of the development of capitalism.

Class Ideology in Science

The fact that a particular class takes the leading part in the general development of science also places definite conditions and limits upon the development of the ideas of science.

On the basis of the material conditions of existence of a class, preconceptions are formed which determine the character of the class ideology. These preconceptions are used and applied, in one way or another, by the intellectual representatives of the class in every sphere of their ideological activity. And so they are used and applied in scientific work, penetrate into and impose themselves upon the theory of the sciences, and in that way influence and colour the entire development of the sciences in each particular period.

In slave society, for example, the idea was developed, and it was more fully worked out in feudal society, that everything which existed constituted a hierarchy, stretching down from God, through various grades of inferior intelligences, to the grades of men, animals, plants and minerals. Everything existed for a purpose, corresponding to its place in the system, and this was what determined its essential properties as well as its movements and changes. This type of conception dominated the sciences. Every theory concerning man or nature had to be formulated in terms of it and made to fit in with it.

For example, it was considered that the heavens beyond the circle of the moon were of a superior nature, belonged to a superior grade of being, to the earth beneath. Hence the heavenly movements (which were supposed to be necessarily circular, because such movements were supposed to be the most perfect) were considered to be movements obeying different laws from earthly ones. Earthly bodies naturally tended to fall towards the centre, which accounted for gravitation as observed on the earth; but this did not apply in the heavens. Such ideas were expressed in the Ptolemaic conception of the base earth at the centre of the universe, with the sun and stars circling beyond it. Copernicus, putting the sun at the centre and making the earth one of the planets, effected a decisive break with this type of conception, and paved the way for the Newtonian conception of universal gravitation and the laws of motion, which subsumed the movements of all the bodies in the universe under one universal scheme of mechanical causality.

Bourgeois ideology in general and bourgeois science in particular attacked and in the end largely got rid of the old, traditional conceptions. This attack arose from and developed on the basis of the growth of the bourgeois social relations. What took the place of the old conceptions were new and typically bourgeois conceptions—conceptions of the basic qualitative identity of all material beings, and of mechanical causality. At the same time, apart from its most radical representatives, the bourgeoisie by no means threw over the conceptions of God and of spirit. But in place of the single graded hierarchy of being, from the basest sort of material being at the bottom to the highest sort of spiritual being (or God) at the top, there was introduced the division of the universe into two totally different spheres—material being subject to fixed, deterministic laws on the one hand, and God and the spiritual world on the other hand.

In one way or another such bourgeois conceptions have

entered into the whole theoretical fabric of modern science, as slave and feudal conceptions did of ancient and medieval science. But there is this important difference—that whereas the old conceptions were hostile to the exploration of nature by experimental methods, the new conceptions were favourable to it and demanded it.[1]

Discovery and Preconception

Because of this class ideological influence in scientific theory, a distinction is always arising in the development of the sciences between the discoveries which science makes and the preconceptions which science takes over and uses.

A discovery is made when, as a result of investigations, something becomes known about the kinds of things which exist, their properties, interconnections and laws. But discoveries must always be expressed in propositions formulated with the aid of definite concepts, and such propositions are always made to form part of a general theory. Considering, therefore, the sum total of the ideas and theories of the sciences at any time, we find that, in one aspect, they consist of the formulation of actual discoveries, and in another aspect, they consist of the general preconceptions in terms of which the discoveries are formulated and knitted together into a general theory.

This distinction between discovery and preconception, which is always present in science, frequently gives rise to a contradiction between discovery and preconception. And this contradiction is continually at work in the development of the sciences.

This contradiction is in essence a contradiction between content and form in science—a contradiction between the actual content of the discoveries of science and the theoretical forms in which they are expressed and generalised. It can work out in either of two ways, a positive way or a negative way. Positively, new discoveries help to shatter old preconceptions and to lead to new ways of understanding things. Negatively,

[1] See S. Mason, *A History of the Sciences*, London, 1953.

the retention of old preconceptions hinders the advance to new discoveries.

For example, at the dawn of modern natural science the old preconceptions were hindering the advance to new discoveries—as when the notion that heavenly motions were completely different from earthly ones hindered the advance of astronomy and mechanics. And then the new discoveries in astronomy and mechanics, when they were realised, helped to shatter the old conceptions and to lead the way to a new outlook.

Again, in modern, bourgeois natural science a contradiction has arisen between the discoveries of science and the traditional, bourgeois mechanistic-metaphysical method of interpreting them.

Thus Engels pointed out that the cumulative effect of the discoveries of modern natural science is to show " that in the last resort nature works dialectically and not metaphysically. . . . But the naturalists who have learned to think dialectically are few and far between, and this conflict of the results of discovery with preconceived modes of thinking explains the endless confusion now reigning in theoretical natural science."[1]

On the one hand, this contradiction leads to " endless confusion " in science, which holds up the advance of science. In biology, for example, extremely rigid mechanistic ideas about living processes were imposed and, when these created difficulties, recourse was had to mystical ideas about life forces, resulting in a sterile controversy between " mechanism " and " vitalism ". Again, when modern discoveries in physics upset the traditional scheme of mechanistic causality, it was claimed that the whole idea of causality had broken down and that " no picture " could be given of fundamental physical processes. On the other hand, the accumulation of discoveries has led to new ways of thinking, to the supplanting of bourgeois ideology by dialectical materialism. Thus Lenin concluded from his examination of new developments in physics : " Modern physics is in travail, it is giving birth to dialectical materialism."[2]

[1] Engels, *Socialism, Utopian and Scientific*, ch. 3.
[2] Lenin, *Materialism and Empirio-Criticism*, ch. 5, section 8.

Social Science

So far we have discussed only the natural sciences. But there is also social science.

The development of natural sciences, which carry out investigations into the properties and laws of natural phenomena, has ultimately been determined by production. That of social science, on the other hand, which carries out investigations into the properties and laws of social phenomena, has been determined by the class struggle. Social science has its roots in the experience of various classes gained in the course of their class struggle.

Sciences always arise from some need. It is in the last analysis the needs of production which call forth natural sciences, and their investigations are carried out on behalf of whatever class is directing production. In turn, the needs of the general management and control of social affairs call forth social science. And its investigations are carried out on behalf of whatever class is either actually managing and controlling social affairs or is struggling to secure such management and control.

The investigation of social phenomena has had considerable development during slave, feudal and capitalist society. The most painstaking investigations have been made into the various different forms of society and of government, and into the social laws which any government must take cognisance of, as well as the investigations of historians, which have established the sequence of public events in the history of various communities.

But up to the emergence of the modern working class, these investigations have been carried out by representatives of exploiting classes. And so it has been primarily the lessons and conclusions about man and society drawn by the exploiting classes which have been incorporated into social science. This has given social science a character profoundly different from natural science. As developed by representatives of exploiting classes, social science—which deals with men's relations and interactions with one another—has been completely separated from natural science—which deals with external nature and man's action on nature. And it has proved impossible to establish the basis of a trustworthy science of society in the way that the same classes have been able to do in the case of external nature.

There are four principal features of social science which have fundamentally distinguished it from natural science.

(1) Class interests absolutely prohibit certain investigations and discoveries in social science, in a way they do not do in natural science. The fact that social science has been developed by exploiting classes as an aid to their class struggles sets impassible limits on the possibilities of discovery by social science—so long as it remains in the hands of those classes.

Thus Stalin, referring specially to economic investigations, wrote : " Unlike the laws of natural science, where the discovery and application of a new law proceeds more or less smoothly, the discovery and application of a new law in the economic field, affecting as it does the interests of the obsolescent forces of society, meets with the most powerful resistance on their part."[1]

It is true, of course, that various discoveries about nature have been resisted for a time by representatives of the ruling classes, for their own ideological reasons. And in this respect the path of the natural sciences has sometimes been anything but " smooth ". Such was the case, for example, with Galileo, or more recently Darwin, or more recently still Michurin. But invariably, in the end, the facts themselves compel recognition, the discoveries are assimilated and used, and the ideologies adapt themselves to the new discoveries. But in the social field, on the other hand, resistance is absolute. An exploiting class will not recognise facts and laws about society if this would fatally prejudice its class interests. It will not recognise facts which would expose the real nature of its own system of exploitation, and laws which would make clear the inevitable downfall of that system.

(2) While exploiting classes have developed the natural

[1] Stalin, *Economic Problems of Socialism in the U.S.S.R.*

sciences as instruments of men's collective mastery over nature, they have not developed social science correspondingly as an instrument of men's collective mastery over their own social organisation. The exploiting classes have developed social sciences only as an instrument to help them secure and maintain their own class rule. Many investigations about society have been undertaken, from which theoretical and practical conclusions have been drawn. But in contrast to the investigations and conclusions of the natural sciences, these have never enabled people to secure such control over the results of their actions that they could direct and plan their co-operative efforts to the realisation of definite ends.

Exploiting classes have been interested in developing instruments of production which have been the means for people's establishing and increasing their mastery over nature. And so, under the patronage of these classes, the natural sciences have more and more helped to realise man's mastery over nature. But at the same time, the development of private property and exploitation has made people subject to effects of their own social relations which lie beyond their conscious social control. And this must be so for as long as exploitation continues to exist. Hence the very same historical process which creates for the exploiting classes the possibility of developing a natural science which helps to realise man's mastery over nature, withholds from them the possibility of developing a social science which helps to realise man's mastery over his own social organisation.

(3) While exploiting classes have been able to develop further and further the scientific investigation not only of the surface phenomena of nature but of the underlying causes and laws of these phenomena, their social science is never able to penetrate to the basic causes and laws of the movement of society.

The basic causes and laws of the movement of society lie in the sphere of the production relations, of the property and class relations. But it is impossible to carry through to the end a scientific investigation in this sphere without finally exposing the truth about the basis of the privileged position of the exploiting classes, and the contradictory and transitory nature of the system of exploitation, which these classes are vitally concerned to hide and disguise. Hence even when, during a progressive phase, the social science of an exploiting class begins to make a more profound analysis of the economic basis of society (as with the British bourgeoisie in the initial phase of industrial capitalism), the class soon falls back from its own achievement, and its social investigations revert to a superficial descriptive level, replete with misleading ideas. The sociologists of exploiting classes can in the end never rightly classify, analyse and explain the phenomena investigated, and constantly introduce illusory motives and false explanations into their accounts of society.

(4) In the hands of the exploiting classes, social science has remained far more profoundly under the influence of class ideology than the natural sciences. In the natural sciences, class ideological preconceptions have often hindered but in the end not prevented the sciences from discovering many of the objective laws and essential interconnections of the phenomena they were investigating. In social science, on the other hand, the general theory of society has been primarily determined by class ideological preconceptions.

Because class interests prohibit certain investigations and discoveries; because the classes in charge of social science cannot develop it as a means towards man's mastery over his own social organisation and so submit its conclusions to the test of social practice; because social science draws back from investigating the basic causes and laws of the movement of society—it follows that the general conceptions of society employed in social science are not derived from scientific investigation but have the character of false consciousness, of class ideological illusion. Consequently, the investigations and conclusions of social science have tended, in the hands of representatives of exploiting classes, to develop primarily as a mere elaboration of class ideological preconceptions—as a classifying and interpreting of social facts in such a way as to reinforce a given class's illusions about society, and to provide arguments to support its political policies.

For all these reasons, therefore, social science in the hands of representatives of exploiting classes has not attained, and never could attain, the same scientific status as the natural sciences. And it has constantly tended to degenerate into mere ruling class apologetics.

The Social Functions of Science

We shall sum up this chapter with some conclusions about the nature of science and the part it plays in social life, in economic and cultural development. Then in the next chapter we shall consider some of the general features of the historical development of science, and the part it is destined to play in the future, in the construction of socialist society.

The distinction between scientific and illusory modes of consciousness is dependent on the different methods of forming ideas about things—on the one hand, forming ideas on the basis of practical interaction with things, developing them by systematic investigation and testing them continually in practice ; on the other hand, proceeding from ideological preconceptions.

These two modes of consciousness are not mutually exclusive. They are opposites, but they interpenetrate. They are opposite tendencies at work in the total development of social consciousness, which interpenetrate at every stage, and which together determine the actual formation of the ideas entertained about nature and society, and about particular aspects of nature and society. And this in turn gives rise to continual contradictions in such ideas. As we have seen, the scientific mode of consciousness has gradually become the predominant influence in the formation of ideas about nature, while the illusory mode of consciousness has remained the predominant influence in the formation of ideas about society.

Scientific investigation and discovery is bound up with social practice, with the practice of production and with the practice of the class struggle. In the last analysis, it always arises from and is governed by the requirements of practice. And meeting the requirements of practice, it makes an essential contribution to practice.

Scientific investigation and discovery plays an indispensable part in the development of the forces of production; and the higher the development of the forces of production the greater and the more necessary is the part played by science in their development. For example, science played no part in the forces of production in the Stone Age. It began to play a part in the development of agriculture, metalworking, public works. It plays a major part in the modern forces of production, since modern technology would be impossible without science; more than that, it plays a leading part, since scientific research pioneers the way of technological development and leads directly to great revolutions in technology.

Contributing thus to the development of forces of production, science becomes a revolutionising force in society. For it is a principal factor in those advances of the forces of production which bring them into conflict with existing relations of production and thus render necessary and inevitable a change in the whole economic structure of society. This is evident today in the development of physical science, for example. Thus atomic energy production is one of the factors which make the replacement of capitalism by socialism urgently necessary, in order that such production may be fruitfully developed in the service of society.

At the same time, science plays a part in class struggle. The natural sciences play such a part indirectly and as a secondary function, social science directly and as a primary function.

The primary social function of natural science is to assist production. From this follows its secondary function in the class struggle. Definite advances in science and technology serve the interests of definite classes, either in their struggle for power or in the consolidation of their regime when they are in power. Thus, for example, the early advances of modern science and technology served the rising bourgeoisie in two ways—first, by enabling them to increase their wealth and so strengthen their social position; second, ideologically by helping

their struggle against the feudal ideology. And when the bourgeoisie was established in power, science and technology were
powerful aids in consolidating the capitalist regime. Today
they still serve the regime of monopoly capitalism. At the
same time, they are also pressed into the service of the working
class and the cause of socialism, and developed in that service—
in the countries where socialism is being built, as a mainspring
in socialist construction ; and everywhere as part of the essential
equipment of socialist ideology.

Various kinds of social investigation, on the other hand, serve
the class struggle directly, and the requirements of class struggle
provide the principal motivation of such investigations. And
in the case of exploiting classes, this, as we have seen, accounts
for the fact that class ideological illusions play a far greater
part in social than in natural science. The comparative study
of different forms of society and of government, the description
and classification of various forms of social activity, the
investigation of the best way of carrying out various forms
of economic activity—these have been essential occupations of
the various ruling and exploiting classes, which have served
them in planning and directing their activities both in gaining
power and consolidating it, and in developing their class views
in the ideological struggle with other classes. In the class struggle
of the working class, in the struggle for socialism, social science
is for the first time developed as an essential means for finding
out how to transform society ; and in this it for the first time
begins to attain a scientific status equivalent to that of the
natural sciences.

The chief and most essential social function of science is,
then, to be found in the part it plays in the development of
social practice. By carrying on scientific investigations to find
things out and to reach general conclusions on the basis of
what they have found out, people are able to expand and
develop their productive forces, and regulate their social intercourse, their individual and social activities, corresponding to
the level of their productive forces and the consequent character
of their production relations. Thus the development of science

is an essential means to the perfection of human life, serving to increase men's mastery over nature, their social wealth, the scope and power of their activities, their ability to manage their affairs and satisfy their requirements.

This bears on the question, recently raised among Marxists, whether science develops as part of the ideological super-structure on the economic basis of society.

On the one hand, since class ideological preconceptions do enter into science, it is clear that science does include within itself views which arise and develop as a superstructure on an economic basis. Such preconceptions arise precisely as products of a given basis of property and class relations, serve that basis as a means to its consolidation and development, and disappear when that basis disappears. We cannot understand the history of science, or its specific character and contradictions at any particular stage, without taking into account the fact that it is developed by definite classes, whose class preconceptions play an active part in its development.

On the other hand, the content of the discoveries of science is not determined by an economic basis. They are directly connected with needs of production and of the social intercourse consequent on production, reflect objective facts and laws, serve society generally and remain valid for any economic basis.

To take a concrete example, that of quantum physics as it has been developed in bourgeois society today. The discoveries concerning the laws of motion of matter on the sub-atomic level are not an ideological superstructure on the bourgeois economic basis. But the theory that events happen without causes, which has been built around these discoveries, is such a superstructure. Hence in its essential discoveries quantum physics has not developed as a superstructure on an economic basis, but certain temporary features of its general theory have so developed.

So, does science develop as a superstructure? No, but the preconceptions forming part of the superstructure do enter into science and influence its development. They influence its development either positively or negatively, assisting scientific discovery or hindering it—just as, in general, the economic basis of property and class relations may be favourable or unfavourable to the further development of science.

Moreover, it is evident that science itself plays a very important part in the ideological development of society.

Scientifically formed concepts, scientific discoveries, enter into ideologies, and science is a strong and growing influence in the formation of ideologies—which thus, in some of their features, become scientific rather than illusory. The higher the development of science the greater the part it must play in general ideological development.

For example, the conception of the evolution of species through natural selection, the conception of the cell as the unit through which life develops, the conception of the atom, the conception of the earth as part of the solar system within the island universe of the milky way, are all scientifically formed conceptions which have become part of the accepted view of nature in bourgeois society, and so part of the current bourgeois ideology. In general, bourgeois ideology not only penetrates science by imposing preconceptions on it but is also itself penetrated by science, at the same time often seeking to "interpret" and explain away scientific discoveries.

But above all, science plays a part as a weapon of criticism in the development of ideology. New concepts and discoveries of science conflict with existing ideology, and shake its preconceptions and the conclusions derived from them. So when new classes are rising to challenge the sway of the old ruling classes, and new ideas are being opposed to the old ideas, scientific investigation and the conclusions derived from it become a revolutionary weapon of criticism.

Above all, therefore, science plays a progressive and liberating part in social development. Its discoveries enhance men's collective power to satisfy their requirements, and serve as means of enlightenment, dispelling the clouds of error and superstition, and furnishing men with knowledge of nature and of themselves.

Particular classes, and particular nations led by particular classes, have made their contributions to the development of the sciences, temporarily stamping upon them their own peculiar characteristics and limitations, and often, having advanced so far in scientific discovery, drawing back, confusing the theory of science with their own illusions and perverting its uses. But whatever the limitations and setbacks, what has been achieved by one class or nation is taken over and carried on by another. Hence in the history of science there has developed, and is developing, a heritage of human knowledge and power. This is the common heritage of mankind, destined to be used for the emancipation of all the people.

CHAPTER NINE

SCIENCE AND SOCIALISM

While great scientific achievements have been scored by
bourgeois science, the capitalist relations have placed limitations
on the development of the sciences. Under socialism, when
science is developed in the people's service, these limitations
are removed. In particular, with the rise of the working class
struggle for socialism, the science of society is established. In
socialist society the old ideological illusions lose their basis,
and there begins to come into being a universal scientific
ideology.

Achievements of Bourgeois Science

PRIOR to modern capitalist times, the sciences developed
mainly at the most elementary, descriptive and classificatory
level. The discoveries of science, considerable as they were in
certain fields, were piecemeal in character, being concerned
with the properties of particular objects and with particular
laws and conceptions, not yet penetrating to the more general
and fundamental laws or affording any reliable general picture
of the interconnections in nature. Since scientific work was
mainly confined to description and classification, the abstractions and generalisations of the sciences, which constitute the
two other major aspects of scientific work, were of necessity
mainly speculations and guesses. And the general theory of
nature was developed as a part of philosophy and theology, and
embodied all the philosophical and theological illusions of the
times.

It was a feature of science in this stage that it made use of
some extremely primitive conceptions about nature. The
alchemists, for instance, accumulated a considerable store of
knowledge about chemical substances and their combinations,
but their chemical theory was extremely primitive, in the literal

sense that it made use of ideas taken over from primitive times. Such, for example, was their idea that chemical substances were living beings made up of matter and spirit, and also possessing sexual attributes. Again, there was a considerable development of astronomical observation in slave and feudal society, but the cosmological theories about the layout of the universe remained under the influence of primitive ideas.

Engels, in one of his letters, pointed out that there has existed " a prehistoric stock of what we should today call bunk ", which has been drawn on (it is still sometimes drawn on, by the way) for the purposes of men's general conception of nature.

" These various false conceptions of nature", he wrote, " . . . have for the most part only a negative economic basis ; the low economic development of the prehistoric period is supplemented and partially conditioned and even caused by the false conceptions of nature. And even though economic necessity was the main driving force of the progressing knowledge of nature and becomes ever more so, it would surely be pedantic to try to find economic causes for all this primitive nonsense. The history of science is the history of the gradual clearing away of this nonsense or of its replacement by fresh but always less absurd nonsense."[1]

The position was, therefore, that the ideology of the ruling classes imposed a certain philosophical and theological character upon the general theory of the sciences. And at the same time, the relatively low level of economic development brought it about that many primitive and nonsensical conceptions found their place in the theories about particular things. These factors could not but hinder the development of the sciences. They acted as powerful negative factors which had to be swept away before the modern development of science, and of production, could become possible.

Modern natural science arose in the period when the power of the feudal nobility was being broken and the modern European bourgeois nations were being formed. " Natural science developed in the midst of the general revolution and was itself

[1] Engels, *Letter* to C. Schmidt, October 27, 1890.

thoroughly revolutionary," wrote Engels.[1] And the same class forces which were carrying through the revolution carried through the development of sciences. Science appeared as a great force of enlightenment, breaking through past ignorance and superstition. It challenged the old authorities with knowledge based on observation and experiment. The men who laid the foundations of modern natural science were of a very different type from the clerks and monkish scholars of the feudal order. They were intensely interested in the development of industry and trade, in new techniques, in travel and discovery. In their hands the discoveries of science became instruments for improving the conditions of human life.

The rise of new sciences was consequent upon a new development of industry.

" Following the crusades, industry developed enormously and brought to light a quantity of new mechanical (weaving, clockmaking, milling), chemical (dyeing, metallurgy, alcohol), and physical (lenses) facts, and this not only gave enormous material for observation, but also itself provided quite other means for experimenting than previously existed, and allowed the construction of new instruments ; it can be said that really systematic experimental science had now become possible for the first time."[2]

In the modern development of natural science which was thus initiated, the abstractions and hypotheses of the sciences ceased to be mere speculations and guesses, and began to be established as verified scientific truths. Scientific theory began to replace the former coupling of primitive bunk with philosophical and theological speculation. And what made this possible for those now engaged in scientific work was the new equipment which they possessed for accurate observation and controlled experiment, and the fact that scientific theories began to be tested not only by scientific observations and experiments but in the practice of social production. The new successes of natural science were dependent, therefore, on

[1] Engels, *Dialectics of Nature*, Introduction.
[2] Engels, *loc. cit.*, Notes.

advancing technology in social production and the social utilisation of science as a force of production.

From this starting point, modern bourgeois natural science has gone on to score great achievements.

(1) There has been achieved what Engels called "the successive development of the separate branches of natural science"[1]—the evolution of the different sciences one from another, and their differentiation one from another. In this process, the successes scored in one field have created the possibility of beginning the scientific investigation of new fields. The whole process has unfolded out of the development of the productive forces of capitalist society, which at one and the same time have presented new problems for science to tackle and provided the technical means for tackling them.

(2) In all the successive fields of science there have been major achievements of analysis—the analysis of the phenomena of nature into their parts or elements, the demonstration of the properties, interconnections and laws of motion of the parts, and so of the laws of motion of the whole. And at the same time as this analysis of nature has been carried out there has been carried out a process of generalisation, demonstrating how the most diverse properties and motions of things are all the consequences of the operation of very general, universally applicable, laws.

(3) A third major achievement of modern natural science has been the discovery of the laws of change and development in nature.

In the initial period of modern natural science the view prevailed that, despite ceaseless changes and interactions, nature in its main features always remained exactly the same. "The planets and their satellites, once set in motion by the mysterious 'first impulse', circled on and on in their pre-destined ellipses for all eternity. . . . The stars remained for ever fixed and immovable in their places. . . . The earth had persisted without alteration. . . . The five continents of the present day had always existed. . . . The species of plants and

[1] *Ibid.*

animals had been established once and for all when they came into existence. . . . All change, all development in nature was denied."[1] But the successive discoveries of the sciences—in astronomy and cosmogony, in physics, in chemistry, in geology and in the biological sciences—shattered this whole picture of the fixity of nature. It was demonstrated that nature in all its parts changes and develops. And this conclusion emerged not as a general speculation—such as had been put forward, for instance, in ancient Greek philosophy—but as a result of detailed investigations, of the analysis of the various processes of nature and the discovery of their laws and interconnections.

(4) Finally, from the discoveries of the natural sciences there has gradually emerged a knowledge of nature which is at once general and detailed—general, in the sense that it embraces the main processes which take place in nature and their interconnections ; and detailed, in the sense that it embraces particular laws and interconnections of things. And this knowledge to an increasing degree has enabled the sciences to give an account of natural processes entirely based on and tested in the investigation of those processes themselves.

" We have arrived at the point ", wrote Engels, " where we can demonstrate as a whole the interconnection between the processes in nature not only in particular spheres but also in the interconnection of these particular spheres themselves, and so can present in an approximately systematic form a comprehensive view of the interconnection in nature by means of the facts provided by empirical natural science itself."[2]

As a result, scientific knowledge of nature gradually supplants philosophical speculation about nature. The account which is given both of particular processes and of their general interconnection is based on and tested in detailed investigations, and not arrived at by philosophical deductions or imaginative guesses.

Formerly, as Engels observed, a " comprehensive view " of nature could be arrived at " only by putting in place of the real

---

[1] Engels, *loc. cit.*, Introduction.
[2] Engels, *Ludwig Feuerbach*, ch. 2.

but as yet unknown interconnections ideal and imaginary ones, filling out the missing facts by figments of the mind and bridging the actual gaps merely in imagination." But once scientific investigations have supplied the missing facts, such a procedure becomes " not only superfluous, but a step back-wards."[1]

Of course, many gaps remain ; and though they keep on being filled, gaps will always remain. Indeed, the filling in of one gap often reveals new and hitherto unsuspected ones. Yet even by the latter part of the last century science had discovered enough to discredit the old type of philosophical-theological account of nature. It has become clear that missing knowledge must always be supplied by pushing on with scientific investigation and not by any other means.

Limitations of Bourgeois Science

The sciences, by assisting in the development of industry and trade, have played an indispensable part in making possible the establishment and development of the capitalist mode of production. But the establishment of the capitalist mode of production has then set limits upon the further development of the sciences.

The great achievement of capitalism is to have transformed small-scale individual production into large-scale social produc-tion, which is able to harness natural forces and make use of modern mechanical instruments of production. The growth of social production—above all in industry, since agriculture remained relatively backward—brought about, and was assisted by, an unprecedented growth of the sciences. In field after field discoveries were made, new sciences were established and developed rapidly, nature gave up her secrets to man and the principles were established for correctly understanding the laws and interconnections of natural processes.

But social production was directed to definite capitalist ends. It was capital which exercised the controlling and directing function in social production. The co-operation in labour,

[1] *Ibid.*

which is the essential feature of social production, was not brought about by the labourers themselves but by the capital which employed and exploited them. It was "not their own act but the act of the capital which brings and keeps them together. . . . The directing motive, the end and aim of capitalist production is to extract the greatest possible amount of surplus value, and consequently to exploit labour-power to the greatest possible extent."[1]

Marx regarded science as a distinct but necessary part of the production process in modern society. Social labour, he observed, includes labour of two kinds. First there is the scientific side, involving the scientific mastery of materials and processes, issuing in inventions and discoveries which improve the existing instruments of production and create new ones. This he termed "universal labour". And secondly, there is co-operative labour itself, the co-operation of workers in utilising the instruments of production.[2]

In capitalist production these two kinds of labour are separated, and both compelled to serve capital. Co-operative labour is the source of surplus value, and the labourer is simply "a hand" to work under the direction of the capitalist, or his managers, for the profit of the capitalist. Advances in production technique are made and applied not because they lighten labour or help to satisfy human needs but because and in so far only as they yield an increased profit. And therefore science, the theory of production, does not develop as an adjunct and instrument of social labour but as an adjunct and instrument of capital which exploits labour-power and directs production towards capitalist profit.

"The labourer is brought face to face with the intellectual potencies of the material process of production, as the property of another, and as a ruling power," wrote Marx. "Modern industry . . . makes science a productive force distinct from labour and presses it into the service of capital."[3]

[1] Marx, *Capital*, Vol. I, ch. 13.
[2] See Marx, *loc. cit.*, Vol. III, ch. 5, section 5.
[3] Marx, *loc. cit.*, Vol. I, ch. 14, section 5.

At first science could advance with giant strides within the limits of the capitalist relations. For capital needed to penetrate the secrets of the natural processes which it used in its drive for profit, and, realising the vital importance of science, was also willing to encourage research along lines for which no immediate practical application was in sight. Scientists felt themselves free and unfettered; it seemed to them that they were conducting their researches for the sake of humanity, or for knowledge for its own sake, and that society was ready to honour and reward them for their discoveries and to put their discoveries, where circumstances permitted, to practical use. Nevertheless, the reality of this bourgeois freedom of science was that science was working all the time for capital, which relied on its discoveries, inventions and theories to effect those improvements in production which would swell capitalist profit.

With the development of capital to its modern, monopoly stage, however, the direct and open subjugation of science to monopoly capital has gradually come about. This has been aided by the very advance of science itself, which has entailed a great increase in costs and so rendered the sciences almost completely dependent on financing by the monopolies, directly or through the state. Not only the researches, inventions and discoveries of scientists have been pressed into the service of capital, but scientists personally. They have lost their former independent status, and been turned into employees and agents of the monopolies—or of the state, which is itself subjugated to the monopolies. And their work is correspondingly regimented. The effect of this is to disorganise scientific work, which can proceed only in directions which the monopolies will pay for; to pervert it, principally and increasingly for military ends, with the growing evils of secrecy and " security ", police and military supervision, " loyalty " tests and tests of ideological orthodoxy; and finally to make science appear not as a source of strength and hope to humanity but as a menace.

The subjection of science to capital, and latterly to monopoly capital, is equally reflected in the theory of science. From the viewpoint of the capitalist class, science, necessary as it is, has always harboured a dangerous ideological trend. This is because of the materialist tendency of its conclusions, which begin to explain everything in men's experience from the material world alone. The bourgeoisie early began to realise that scientific materialism can be socially subversive, if it begins to submit the foundations of society and of ruling class privilege to scientific criticism, and to show how, armed with science, the people can achieve their emancipation. Hence for a long time philosophical theories have been woven around science, seeking to explain away its radical materialist tendency, and above all seeking to impose limits upon its possible development and application.

Thus it has been laid down that science can only deal with certain aspects of the forces of nature, but not with the under-lying and controlling spiritual forces in the world; that, indeed, it cannot penetrate to the real forces at work in nature, but can only deal with some of their effects; that, finally, it can only record and correlate the sensations which are produced in our minds, while the real world outside remains unknowable and mysterious. Such views about science and in science, which have become extremely widespread in the capitalist world today, were already being developed as long ago as the seventeenth century.[1]

The more the life of society, including science, has come under the domination of the modern monopolies, the more has the dead hand of reactionary theory gripped the sciences. Eminent scientists proclaim that science is compatible with almost any kind of " faith "—except faith in humanity; that the real world is unknowable; that the aim of progress based on scientific knowledge is illusory. Anti-scientific ideas are imported into science, where they are set up as dogmas—unmoved movers, mysterious creation, events without a cause. At the same time, the advance of scientific discovery cannot be halted, and scientists themselves become acutely aware of the

[1] See, for example, Malebranche, *Dialogues on Metaphysics and Religion*, 1688.

restrictions imposed upon them in practice by monopoly interests and in theory by anti-scientific ideas. Many begin to seek the way out, and find it in joining the working-class struggle for a new social order in which science will have unrestricted development in serving the interests of all members of society.

Science for the People

While the aim of capitalist production is capitalist profit, " the aim of socialist production is not profit, but man and his needs, that is, the satisfaction of his material and cultural requirements". This aim is realised " through the continuous expansion and perfection of socialist production on the basis of higher techniques".[1] It is to this aim, therefore, that the development of science is subordinated in socialist society.

In capitalism, the direction of social production is a function of capital, whose aim is maximum capitalist profit. In socialism, on the other hand, the direction of social production becomes a function of social labour itself, the aim of which is maximum satisfaction of the material and cultural requirements of society. The task of developing the theory of production must always be in the same hands as the direction of its practice. In capitalism science is separated from labour and pressed into the service of capital exploiting labour. But in socialism, science becomes united with labour. Socialist science is the scientific department of social labour—in other words, that department which carries out the research, invention and theoretical work necessary continuously to expand and perfect socialist production, and to satisfy the constantly rising material and cultural requirements of socialist society.

Removed from the control of the monopolies and turned into a public concern, the all-round development of science becomes a subject of planning under socialism. This does not mean, of course, that the discoveries to be made over a period are planned in advance, since no one can know what is going to be discovered until the discovery is made. It means that the allocation of the resources and the direction for research in

[1] Stalin, *Economic Problems of Socialism in the U.S.S.R.*

all fields are planned. Such planning entails the combination of short-term and long-term considerations. At one and the same time science concentrates on the solution of immediate practical problems, and undertakes fundamental researches dictated by the requirements of theoretical advance and aspiring to results far beyond current practice.

Scientific workers work in close unity with productive workers. A new type of scientist emerges, recruited from the ranks of the working people. And science, from being the preserve of a single social group associated with the exploiters, eventually becomes the common possession and concern of all. This can only set free immense new forces for scientific work and for the utilisation of its results, and lead to an immense acceleration and expansion of science.

At the same time, the restricting dogmas of bourgeois theory are thrown off. The theory of science is developed in line with its discoveries, on the basis of socialist practice, as a guide to further discovery and practical application, with free discussion and criticism.

At an early stage, before the development of the separate sciences, science was scarcely distinguished from philosophy. One feature of the history of philosophy and of science is the separating of the sciences from philosophy. As sciences branch off from philosophy, general ideas about nature are established on the basis of the scientific investigation of nature. Yet, as we have seen, philosophical ideas continue to penetrate the sciences, influencing particularly the more abstract parts of scientific theory. The emancipation of science from philosophical preconceptions is only completed with the development of science under socialism. For then philosophy ceases to exist in its old form as a theory of the world independent of science and imposing its views on science, but develops as a summation of the principles inherent in scientific thought itself—the principles of logic and dialectics—and therefore as a theoretical instrument and guide in scientific work.

Commenting on the relations of science and philosophy, Engels wrote :

" Natural scientists believe that they free themselves from philosophy by ignoring or abusing it. They cannot, however, make any headway without thought, and for thought they need thought determinations. They take these categories unreflectingly from the common consciousness of so-called educated persons. . . . Hence they are no less in bondage to philosophy, and those who abuse philosophy most are slaves to precisely the worst vulgarised relics of the worst philosophies. . . . Natural scientists allow philosophy to prolong a pseudo-existence by making shift with the dregs of the old metaphysics. Only when natural and historical science has adopted dialectics will all the philosophical rubbish . . . be superfluous, disappearing in positive science."[1]

In socialism alone, moreover, can there be realised the true disinterestedness essential to the fullest development of science.

The process of scientific investigation demands that conclusions shall be drawn on the basis of thorough investigation alone, without consideration for what this or that interest would like to be the case, or this or that school of thought believes. And it demands that every conclusion shall be subject to criticism on the basis of further investigation.

This necessary characteristic of scientific work was repeatedly stressed by Marx. Thus, for example, in contrasting Ricardo's scientific approach in political economy to that of Malthus, he wrote of " Ricardo's inconsiderateness " and " scientific honesty ", of " Ricardo's scientific impartiality ", which " comes out just as inconsiderately against the bourgeoisie as in other cases he comes out against the proletariat and the aristocracy". Malthus, on the other hand, committed a " sin against science " by adapting his conclusions to the interests of ruling class apologetics. " The contemptible Malthus draws . . . only those conclusions which are acceptable and useful to the aristocracy as against the bourgeoisie and to both as against the proletariat." He sought to " accommodate science to a point of view not derived from science itself . . . but borrowed

[1] Engels, *Dialectics of Nature*, Notes.

from outside, from extrinsic interests foreign to science".[1]

In society based on exploitation barriers cannot but arise against disinterested inquiry. Investigations are started, but the point comes when stronger and stronger social pressures operate to force many scientists to trim their conclusions to various ideological and political requirements of the ruling class, or even to bring the investigations to a premature end. Only when exploitation of man by man is abolished, and inquiry is consciously directed to the end of making life more abundant for everyone, are all the barriers to disinterested inquiry thrown down. For then the very interest which promotes inquiry—that is to say, the common interest in obtaining reliable knowledge as a means to life—demands that nothing shall stand in the way of prosecuting inquiries to the end.

Of course, the old habit of demanding that investigations shall prove what some particular group wishes to be proved, and of objecting to any questioning of certain conclusions, is one which dies hard. The development of socialism, on the other hand, demands that science shall be truly disinterested, and shall carry on its inquiries without consideration for what any particular person or persons have asserted or wish to be believed. " It is generally recognised that no science can develop and flourish without a battle of opinions, without freedom of criticism," wrote Stalin.[2] " Science is called science just because it does not recognise fetishes, just because it does not fear to raise its hand against the obsolete and antiquated, and because it lends an attentive ear to the voice of experience, of practice."[3]

In general, socialism sets science free from all the limitations and restrictions hitherto imposed on its development. Just as the socialist ownership of the means of production removes the fetters imposed on the development of production by private ownership and appropriation, and renders possible the un-restricted development of production to satisfy people's needs,

[1] Marx, *Theories of Surplus Value*. Quoted from R. L. Meek, *Marx and Engels on Malthus*, New York, 1954

[2] Stalin, *Concerning Marxism in Linguistics*.

[3] Stalin, *Speech at First All-Union Conference of Stakhanovites*.

so does it remove the fetters imposed on the development of the sciences. The methods of scientific investigation are no different under socialism from capitalism ; for these methods, gradually perfected during the successive stages of economic development, are not the product of any particular system. The point is that the economic, political and ideological factors hindering their application are removed.

From socialism, wrote Engels, " will date a new epoch in history, in which mankind itself, and with mankind all branches of its activity, and especially natural science, will experience an advance that will put everything preceding it in the deepest shade".[1]

The Science of Society

Bourgeois science could penetrate deeply into the laws of natural processes because the bourgeoisie needed such knowledge for the sake of its profits. The capitalists do not want fairy stories about electricity, for example, but knowledge of its real laws (although their ideology still impels them to believe not a few fairy stories). But as regards the laws of social development, the capitalists, though they can use masses of superficial data about society, can never recognise them. For to do so would lead straight to the conclusion of the fall of themselves and their whole system.

Unlike the natural sciences, therefore, the placing of social science on a firm basis, the discovery of the fundamental laws of development of society, only begins with the beginning of the struggle for socialism, and continues only in association with that struggle and then with the actual building of socialist society. The science of society develops as the scientific theory guiding the working class struggle for socialism. It arises and develops as the theoretical basis for the social conceptions of the working class.

Bourgeois social science reached its highest development in the work of the British investigators Adam Smith and David Ricardo, whose inquiry into the laws of the production and

[1] Engels, *loc. cit.* Introduction.

distribution of the means of subsistence in human society laid the foundations for the science of political economy, the science of the economic basis of society. These investigations were undertaken to serve the needs of management of nascent capitalist economy. But the conditions of development of capitalist rule and capitalist exploitation inhibited any further scientific advance by bourgeois investigators. They could not go on, as Marx did, to uncover, by the discovery of surplus value, the secret of capitalist exploitation.

Subsequent bourgeois economics, and bourgeois social science generally, has busied itself with the accumulation of a vast array of facts and correlations of facts. It has also accumulated a considerable amount of practical knowledge about how to operate the capitalist system. But it has sedulously avoided investigation into the real relations of production on which those facts are based and from which alone they can be understood, substituting superficial or false explanations.

What Marx said of " vulgar " bourgeois economics can be said of bourgeois social science generally. It " deals with appearances only . . . seeks plausible explanations of the most obtrusive phenomena for bourgeois daily use, but for the rest confines itself to systematising in a pedantic way, and proclaiming for everlasting truths, the trite ideas held by the self-complacent bourgeoisie with regard to their own world, to them the best of all possible worlds".[1] And with such science, " it was no longer a question whether this theorem or that was true, but whether it was useful to capital or harmful, expedient or inexpedient, politically dangerous or not. In place of disinterested inquirers, there were hired prize-fighters ; in place of genuine scientific research, the bad conscience and the evil intent of apologetics."[2]

So while there are bourgeois investigations establishing numerous facts and a few isolated and superficial laws of social science, there is, and can be, no bourgeois science of society embracing the fundamental laws, but only the Marxist, socialist

[1] Marx, *Capital*, ch. 1, section 4 (footnote).
[2] Marx, *loc. cit.*, Preface to 2nd edition.

science of society. Marx's discoveries about the fundamental laws of social development were possible only because he took up a standpoint against capitalist society, and recognised the revolutionary role of the working class and the necessity of the replacement of capitalism by socialism. With them, he established the basis of social science as Galileo and Newton of physical science, or Schwann and Darwin of biological science.

The End of the Old Ideology

Because the socialist movement develops scientific conceptions of society, of social relations and the laws of social development, it follows that it opposes and begins to destroy ideological illusions.

The socialist movement opposes scientific ideas to the ideological preconceptions of the exploiting classes. In other words, in the struggle for socialism scientific ideas are pitted against the old illusions. The aim of society without exploitation, whose basic law of development is the maximum satisfaction of the material and cultural needs of the people, carries with it the struggle to end ideological illusions of all kinds and to supplant them by science—in other words, to develop a universal scientific ideology.

Instead of developing a false consciousness, the struggle for socialism requires the endeavour to conceive things as they are and not in fantastic connections. Instead of employing illusory ideas to disguise real social relations and real social motives to serve the exploitation of one class by another, it requires true ideas to serve the ending of all exploitation and the satisfaction of the needs of the whole of society.

In the struggle under capitalism, the working class party must continually fight to eradicate the influence of capitalist ideology in its own ranks and among the working people, to base its whole policy, mass work and propaganda on the scientific theory of Marxism-Leninism and to educate the whole movement in this theory. Unlike the views of the exploiting classes, the view of society of the working class, which serves the working class struggle, does not, and cannot, arise and develop spontaneously as a class ideology, but arises and develops as a science.

And when the working class has conquered power and is leading in the building of socialist society, then the task is posed of finally eradicating all the hangovers of the old ideology from all departments of social life. From ideological misconception, society as a whole must advance to a scientific outlook.

This advance is possible and necessary because the ideologies of the old society based on exploitation, with their false consciousness and mystification, lose their basis when socialism comes into being.

In socialism, property in the means of production is public or co-operative property, and production is consciously regulated and planned. For what sort of ideas, then, does socialist economy provide the basis? Precisely for scientific ideas, developing through the extension of scientific understanding of man and his conditions of life. Such ideas alone can serve the consolidation and development of the socialist economic basis. For this end cannot be served by ideas which mystify and delude people. Its success requires knowledge of the laws of nature and society, and a social consciousness informed by such knowledge.

In so far, therefore, as other modes of consciousness persist in socialist society, they are merely hangovers from the old conditions, injurious to the consolidation and development of the socialist system. They must therefore be actively combated, and eventually must give way and disappear before the new scientific socialist consciousness.

The illusions which last longest are those of religion—these being also the oldest. For so long as numbers of people remain comparatively poor and ignorant, some basis remains for religious illusions. Moreover, a religious form can be given also to socialist strivings ; and in this respect religion can, under certain conditions, play even a subsidiary positive role in the building of socialism, as we see in the case of the reformed churches in socialist countries.

" The religious reflex of the real world can, in any case,

only finally vanish", wrote Marx, " when the practical relations of everyday life offer to man none but perfectly intelligible and reasonable relations with regard to his fellow men and nature.

" The life process of society, which is based on the process of material production, does not strip off its mystical veil until it is treated as production by freely associated men, and is consciously regulated by them in accordance with a settled plan."[1]

When the life process of society is indeed carried on by freely associated men in accordance with a settled plan, and when in consequence men are involved in none but perfectly intelligible and reasonable relations with their fellow men and nature, then, naturally enough, there is no basis left for any illusions about the conditions of human life, for any mystification, and human consciousness finally sheds such mystification and illusions.

Scientific Foundations of Socialist Consciousness

The new socialist consciousness, which is achieved as a universal mode of consciousness in socialist society, is the consciousness of new socialist people—of working people who have never known exploitation and who are masters of their country, who live by co-operation and are free of the selfish individualism of the private property owner. The conscious existence of such people requires no ideological illusions. On the contrary, it requires a clear, unclouded consciousness, constantly enriched and developed as a result of free inquiry, discussion and criticism.

This presupposes knowledge of society and its laws, and of how to utilise those laws in the interests of society; and knowledge of nature and of how to make it serve man—both constituting parts of a single developing whole of scientific knowledge.

In socialist society, natural and social science are no longer divorced. " Only if science starts from nature is it real science," wrote Marx. " . . . History itself is a real part of natural

[1] Marx, loc. cit., Vol. I, ch. I, section 4.

history, of the development of nature into man. Later natural science will include the science of man in the same way as the science of man will include natural science. There will be only one science."[1]

In this " one science ", Marx observed, " man " or society, becomes " the object of material consciousness " ; that is to say, the conception of man and society loses its former illusory ideological character, and is as scientifically based as the conception of nature. And similarly, " the higher needs of ' man as man ' become real needs " ; that is to say, in place of illusory ideas concerning " the higher needs of man ", which in fact express the ideology of exploiting classes who stifle the satisfaction of the real needs of the masses, the conception of man's needs is based on his real needs. These real needs which develop on the basis of the material life of society include far more than elementary physical needs, since from this basis arise the needs of culture, knowledge and fellowship.

The essential feature of " man as man ", of man as distinct from the animal, is the creation and satisfaction of his own needs through the social mastery of nature. In society based on exploitation, the mass of people are producing for the benefit of others, not for themselves ; only their minimum physical or animal needs are satisfied ; hence they are denied a properly human existence, and, as a compensation, their " higher needs " are represented as belonging to some spiritual life, divorced from material life. In socialist society, when exploitation of man by man is abolished, the whole of men's requirements, material and spiritual, can be understood as arising from their co-operative mastery of nature, and as being satisfied on the basis of the continuous expansion and perfection of social production.

As a result of the development of socialism, therefore, it eventually comes about that science plays the determining part in forming people's whole outlook. People will then have made themselves free to build up knowledge and control of all the aspects of their lives, for the sake of welfare and happiness and of realising the fullness of life.

[1] Marx, *Economic-Philosophical Manuscripts.*

Part Three

TRUTH AND FREEDOM

CHAPTER TEN

TRUTH

Truth is correspondence between ideas and objective reality. Such correspondence is usually only partial and approximate. The truth we can establish always depends on our means for discovering and expressing truth, but at the same time the truth of ideas, though relative in this sense, depends on the objective facts to which ideas correspond. We can never attain complete, full, absolute truth, but are always advancing towards it.

Absolute and Partial Truth

WE have seen that in the development of our ideas all kinds of illusions arise, but also truth. What, then, is truth ? It is correspondence between ideas and objective reality.

Such correspondence between our ideas and reality is only gradually established, and then the correspondence is often no more than partial and incomplete. For an idea may not in all respects correspond to its object but may correspond only partially ; and there may be much in the object which is not reproduced in the idea at all, so that the idea and its correspondence to the object are incomplete. In such cases, we should not say that our idea was false, but yet it would not be absolutely —completely and in all respects—true. Truth, therefore, is not a property which an idea, or a proposition, either possesses or does not possess ; it may belong to an idea to a certain degree, within certain limits, in certain respects.

Of course, there can be no doubt that some propositions are indeed absolutely true : they are quite well enough established for us to be able confidently to assert this.

This applies, for example, to many statements of particular facts. These facts were the case, and consequently the propositions which state them are true, absolutely true, and always will be true without modification. William the Conqueror did in fact invade England in the year 1066 : therefore the proposition asserting that fact is an absolute truth.

And certain general statements, too, are absolutely true. Lenin instanced two of them—people cannot live without eating, and platonic love alone will not beget babies.[1] These general statements correspond to facts, and their correspondence is absolute. And there are plenty more such general statements whose title to absolute truth need never be questioned.

But most of the statements which we make cannot be said in this way to be absolutely true. For we do not in general confine our statements to " truisms " and to the bald assertion of well-established facts. Most of the statements we make, whether statements of particular facts or of general conclusions, may be true enough for certain purposes but yet not be absolutely true, in the sense of an absolute correspondence between statement and reality. On the contrary, they require to be corrected, improved upon, restated in the light of new experience and new knowledge. But they are not for that reason untrue : they are partial, relative, approximate truths.

This characteristic of truth—that it is for the most part partial and not absolute, approximate and not exact, provisional and not final—is very well known to science. The laws which science establishes certainly reflect objective processes ; they correspond to the real motion and interconnection of things in the external world. Yet science has established few laws which can claim to be absolute truths.

For example, the laws of classical mechanics, which formulate the principles of the mechanical interactions of bodies and are continually and confidently employed in all kinds of engineering projects, are now known not to correspond to the movement of matter on a sub-atomic scale. In other words, they are not absolute truths. But we do not for that reason hold that classical mechanics is now shown to be false. Quantum mechanics provides a better approximation than classical mechanics, because its laws not only correspond to the movement of matter on a sub-atomic scale but also include the laws of classical

[1] Lenin, *Materialism and Empirio-Criticism*, ch. 3, section 5.

mechanics as limiting cases; but even so, no scientist would claim that quantum mechanics either was an absolute truth.

In general, science has no interest in absolute truth. Indeed, if once any proposition is asserted as an absolute truth, there is an end of all further inquiry: if absolute truth is attained, then there is no room for further investigation. The claim to establish absolute truth is therefore actually antithetical to science, since such a claim must prevent us from carrying on further investigation, from advancing our knowledge, from proceeding from less approximate to more approximate truth, in other words, from pursuing science.

"Really scientific works therefore as a rule avoid such dogmatic and moral expressions as error and truth," wrote Engels, "while these expressions meet us everywhere in works . . . in which empty phrasemongering attempts to impose on us as the sovereign result of sovereign thought."[1]

Truth and Error

If we recognise that, outside a very limited field of statements of undoubted fact, the truth of every statement is partial, approximate and provisional only, then it follows that we must always be prepared to correct and modify our statements in the light of new experience.

But more than that. When new experiences arise, calling for the correction and modification of certain statements, then to persist in still asserting them in their old, unmodified form means that they turn from truth into falsehood in the new conditions.

For example, the laws of classical mechanics are still as true as ever they were for most engineering purposes, and no one proposes to dispense with them and reject them as false. Nevertheless, since experience has shown that they do not hold without modification for all known movements of matter, it follows that to assert the Newtonian laws as applying without qualification to all matter in motion would be to assert an untruth.

An approximate and partial truth, which is true enough

[1] Engels, *Anti-Dühring*, Part I, ch. 9.

within certain limits, can become, therefore, an untruth if it is applied beyond those limits.

Again, Marx and Engels stated that when socialist society was established, then the state would eventually wither away. This was and is true—but not without qualification. Marx and Engels could not state the qualification, because they lacked the necessary experience. But the experience of building socialism in one country, the Soviet Union, has shown that so long as socialist and capitalist countries continue to co-exist the state must remain in being in socialist countries ; only when socialism is established on a world scale can the state begin to wither away. It follows that to assert now, without qualification, that when socialism is established the state will wither away is to assert something false. Indeed, it would be to assert something not merely false but definitely harmful in relation to existing socialist countries : for such an assertion would lead to a lack of concern for strengthening the socialist state, therefore to a possible weakening of the socialist state and to the capitalists taking advantage of this weakening to intervene and overthrow the socialist system.

This shows that, as Engels pointed out, " truth and error, like all concepts which are expressed in polar opposites, have absolute validity only in an extremely limited field . . . As soon as we apply the antithesis between truth and error outside that narrow field . . . both poles of the antithesis change into their opposites, truth becomes error and error truth."[1]

Or as Stalin observed : " Dialectics tells us that nothing in the world is eternal, everything in the world is transient and mutable ; nature changes, society changes, habits and customs change, conceptions of justice change, truth itself changes— that is why dialectics regards everything critically ; that is why it denies the existence of a truth established once and for all."[2]

Just as truths are for the most part only approximate and contain the possibility of being converted into untruths, so are

[1] *Ibid.*
[2] Stalin, *Anarchism or Socialism?* ch. 1.

many errors found to be not absolute falsehoods but to contain a germ of truth.

Whatever people say is said in terms of the experiences and ideas available to them. It follows that while they may be led to make quite erroneous statements, nevertheless it can happen that erroneous statements reflect, though erroneously, something which is actually the case.

For instance, the Puritans in the English Revolution said they were the elect of God. But even this contained a germ of truth—namely, that they were in fact the rising progressive social force which was bound to overthrow the decaying forces of the old society. Their ideas about being " the elect of God " were certainly erroneous ; but this was their way of expressing something which was undoubtedly the case.

Similarly many erroneous views in science and philosophy, which have had to be, not modified, but rejected as errors, concealed a certain truth which received in them an erroneous, distorted expression.

In general, errors which are simply plain, downright errors and nothing else—errors which contain no element of truth at all—are less important and are more easily disposed of than errors which have a certain basis in fact. The former can be refuted by pointing to facts which contradict them, or can be exposed as simple nonsense. The latter are apt to be far more influential, and therefore far more dangerous. And to refute such errors, it is necessary not simply to reject them and sweep them aside but to show how the truth is distorted in them and to re-state that truth free of distortion.

This illustrates what Lenin meant when he wrote of idealist philosophy :

" Philosophical idealism is only nonsense from the standpoint of crude, simple, metaphysical materialism. On the other hand, from the standpoint of dialectical materialism, philosophical idealism is a one-sided, exaggerated . . . development . . . of one of the features, sides, facets of knowledge into an absolute, divorced from matter, from nature, apotheosised. Idealism is clericalism. True. But philosophical idealism is . . . a road to clericalism through one of the shades of the infinitely complex knowledge . . . of man. . . . It is not groundless; it is a sterile flower undoubtedly, but it is a sterile flower that grows on the living tree of . . . human knowledge."[1]

We should recognise, then, that certain erroneous views, including idealist views, could represent, in their time, a contribution to truth—since they were, perhaps, the only ways in which certain truths could first begin to come to expression. But that does not mean that we need have the slightest use for such erroneous views, once their erroneousness can be detected. Idealists made a contribution to philosophy, for example : but that does not imply that we should have the slightest use for idealist philosophy today, in our present conditions, when such truth as was expressed by idealism can be expressed much better without it, and when the essential distortion and falsehood contained in idealism can be fully exposed.

The Relativity of Truth

We have seen, then, that most truth is approximate, partial and incomplete, and that error is to be found in truth, and truth in error. Hence on any subject we generally possess a measure of truth, but not the absolute truth. The measure of truth about anything which we can achieve at any particular time, and how—in what terms and how adequately—we express it, depends on the means which are available at that time for discovering and expressing truth.

Truth is always relative to the particular means whereby we have arrived at it. We can only express the truth about things in terms of our own experience of them and of the operations whereby we have come to know about them.

But at the same time, this truth does relate to the objective, material world and constitutes an ever more adequate reflection of the real properties and laws of motion of objective things and processes.

Therefore while the form of expression of truth and the limits of its approximation to objective reality depend on us, its

[1] Lenin, *On Dialectics.*

content, what it is about, the objective reality to which it corresponds, does not depend on us.

In this sense there is an element of both relativity and absoluteness, of subjectivity and objectivity, in every truth. Truth is relative inasmuch as it is expressed in terms depending on the particular circumstances, experience and means of arriving at truth of the people who formulate it. It is absolute inasmuch as what is expressed or reproduced in these terms is objective reality, existing independently of men's knowledge of it.

If the side of relativity only is stressed, then there results subjective idealism and relativism, for which truth relates exclusively to our own observations and operations, not to the objective world, the nature of which is said to be unknowable and inexpressible. Sir Arthur Eddington, for example, noting that our knowledge of the atom was mainly derived from observations of pointer readings and flashes on screens—since these were the indications afforded by the apparatus used to explore the atomic world—concluded that we in fact knew nothing about atoms existing in the objective world but only about the " pointer readings and similar indications".[1]

If, on the other hand, only the other side is stressed, the side of absoluteness or objectivity, then what results is dogmatism. Thus earlier physicists, for example, confident that their physical theories did reflect objective material reality, stated that the world consisted of nothing but little, hard particles like microscopic billiard balls, and that no other kind of material reality existed.

Clearly, it is necessary to take into account, both that truth is reflection of objective reality, and that this reflection is at the same time conditioned and limited by the particular circumstances under which it was created.

" For dialectical materialism", wrote Lenin, " there is no impassible boundary between relative and absolute truth. . . . The materialist dialectics of Marx and Engels certainly does contain relativism, but is not reducible to relativism, that is,

[1] See Eddington, *The Nature of the Physical World*, ch. 12.

it recognises the relativity of all our knowledge, not in the sense of the denial of objective truth, but in the sense of the historically conditioned nature of the limits of the approximation of our knowledge of this truth."[1]

Asking " Does objective truth exist ? " Lenin pointed out that two questions must be distinguished and not confounded together :

" (1) Is there such a thing as objective truth, that is, can human ideas have a content that does not depend on a subject, that does not depend either on a human being or on humanity ?

" (2) If so, can human ideas, which give expression to objective truth, express it all at one time, as a whole, unconditionally, absolutely, or only approximately, relatively ? "[2]

The answer to these questions is clear.

(1) Human ideas can, and do, have a content that does not depend either on particular people or on humanity generally, since these ideas reproduce objective reality existing independently of any person's idea of it.

(2) These ideas do not reproduce objective reality in its entirety and with complete faithfulness, but only approximately, and relatively to the way in which people have been able to discover and express truth.

Since truth consists in the correspondence of ideas with objective reality, it is evident that we have always to reckon with both sides of the relationship—the subject as well as the object. On the one hand is objective reality, which depends in no way on the ideas which we may form about it. On the other hand, ideas are formed in the process of human activity and are therefore conditioned by the nature of the activity out of which they are produced. How, in what form, with what approximation, reality is expressed in our ideas depends on us and our activity—that is, on the subjective factor. But that which is expressed in our ideas, their content, what they are about, does not depend on any subjective factor, but constitutes

[1] Lenin, *Materialism and Empirio-Criticism*, ch. 2, section 5.
[2] Lenin, *loc. cit.*, ch. 2, section 4.

an "objectively existing measure or model existing independently of humanity to which our relative knowledge
approximates".[1]

Relative and Absolute Truth : Causality, Space and Time

As an example of how absolute truth is expressed through
relative truth, we can consider the conceptions of causality,
and of space and time.

Our ideas about causality in nature are produced as a result
of our experiences in dealing with natural objects. We learn
from experience that we ourselves can produce changes in
nature in a regulated way, and on this basis we formulate ideas
of causal connections and causal law. Thus the way in which
we come to recognise causality, and the ideas of causal connections which we express from time to time, are subjectively
conditioned. With the development of production and of social
relations and social activities, the conception of causality has
been modified and changed—animism, final causes, mechanical
interaction and dialectical interaction being so many stages in
the development of the idea of causality.

But while our ideas about causality arise from our experience
and depend upon the character of that experience, the existence
of causality in nature is an objective fact, altogether independent
of ourselves and our experience. It is because we, as subjects,
experience our own power to cause changes in external objects,
and similarly experience the compelling power of those objects
upon ourselves, that we first arrive at the idea of causality ;
and that idea is elaborated and developed in relation to the
development of social life. But the reality which corresponds
to this idea, and which is reproduced with a greater or lesser
degree of adequacy in our ideas of causal connections, is an
objective reality, independent of ourselves, independent of any
relationship between subject and object.

Idealism stresses only the subjective side of the idea of
causality. Idealist philosophers have maintained that causality
was invented simply to bring a rational order into our experience

[1] Lenin, *loc. cit.*, ch. 2, section 5.

and that it is then erroneously attributed to the external world independent of experience. But in opposition to idealism, " the recognition of objective law in nature and the recognition that this law is reflected with approximate fidelity in the mind of man is materialism".[1]

It is the same with our conceptions of space and time. Starting with our perceptions of the passage of time and of the spatial characteristics and relations of objects, and with the discovery of methods of expressing the spatial and temporal properties and relations of things by means of measurements, our general conceptions of space and time have been gradually developed and elaborated. The conception of space and time is always relative to human experience, but space and time do not depend on human experience. On the contrary, " the basic forms of all being are space and time ",[2] and human conceptions of space and time are always approximate reflections of the real spatial and temporal forms of the objective world.

" Recognising the existence of objective reality, i.e., matter in motion, independently of our mind, materialism must also inevitably recognise the objective reality of space and time," wrote Lenin. " . . . The mutability of human conceptions of space and time no more refutes the objective reality of space and time than the mutability of scientific knowledge of the structure and forms of matter in motion refutes the objective reality of the external world. . . . It is one thing, how, with the help of various sense-organs, man perceives space, and how, in the course of a long historical development, abstract ideas of space are derived from these perceptions ; it is an entirely different thing whether there is an objective reality independent of mankind which corresponds to these perceptions and conceptions of mankind. . . . Our experience and our perceptions adapt themselves more and more to objective space and time, and reflect them ever more correctly and profoundly."[3]

[1] Lenin, *loc. cit.*, ch. 3, section 3.
[2] Engels, *Anti-Duhring*, Part I, ch. 5.
[3] Lenin, *loc. cit.*, ch. 3, section 5.

The Progress of Truth

How far is the human mind capable of attaining to and establishing truth ?

Complete, full, absolute truth—the whole truth and nothing but the truth about everything—is something we can never attain. But it is something towards which we are always approximating.

We advance towards full, comprehensive truth, embracing not only particular facts but general laws and interconnections, by means of a series of particular, provisional and approximate truths. The truth which can be formulated by any individual, or by mankind at any particular time, is always approximate, incomplete and subject to correction. But individuals learn from each other, both from each other's achievements and from each other's mistakes ; and the same applies to the succeeding generations of society. Therefore the sum of incomplete, particular, provisional and approximate truths is always approaching nearer to but never reaching the goal of complete comprehensive, final and absolute truth.

The world which is reproduced in our ideas and statements really exists. They are true in proportion as they correspond to it and reproduce it correctly. We test this truth in experience, in practice. The correspondence is never complete, exact, absolute. But it continually approaches yet is always infinitely distant from that absolute limit as truth and knowledge continually advance, as men perfect their instruments of production and their means of acquiring knowledge.

Thus Engels wrote :

" The perception that all the phenomena of nature are systematically interconnected drives science on to prove this systematic interconnection throughout, both in general and in detail. But an adequate, exhaustive, scientific statement of this interconnection, the formulation in thought of an exact picture of the world-system in which we live, is impossible for us and will always remain impossible.

" If at any time in the evolution of mankind such a final, conclusive system of the interconnections within the world—

physical as well as mental and historical—were brought to completion, this would mean that human knowledge had reached its limit. . . . Mankind therefore finds itself faced with a contradiction : on the one hand, it has to gain an exhaustive knowledge of the world system in all its inter-relations ; and on the other hand, because of the nature both of man and of the world system, this task can never be com-pletely fulfilled. But this contradiction lies not only in the nature of the two factors—the world and man—it is also the main lever of all intellectual advance, and finds its solution continuously, day by day, in the endless progressive evolution of humanity. . . .

"Each mental image of the world system is and remains in actual fact limited, objectively through the historical stage, and subjectively through the physical and mental constitution of its maker."[1]

Nevertheless through the endless progressive evolution of such limited mental images of the objective world, mankind continually attains more complete truth, more comprehensive knowledge.

"Is human thought sovereign ? " Engels asked, meaning thereby can we achieve the complete truth about everything, can we achieve comprehensive and fully certified knowledge ?

"Before we can answer yes or no we must inquire : what is human thought ? Is it the thought of the individual man ? No. But it exists only as the individual thought of many billions of past, present and future men. . . . In other words, the sovereignty of thought is realised in a series of extremely unsovereignly-thinking human beings ; the knowledge which has an unconditional claim to truth is realised in a series of relative errors ; neither the one nor the other can be fully realised except through an endless eternity of human existence.

"Here again we find the same contradiction as we found above, namely, between the character of human thought, necessarily conceived as absolute, and its reality in individual human beings with their extremely limited thought. This is a

[1] Engels, *Anti-Duhring*, Part I, ch. 3.

contradiction which can only be solved in the infinite progression, or what is for us, at least from a practical standpoint, the endless succession, of generations of mankind. In this sense human thought is just as much sovereign as not sovereign, and its capacity for knowledge just as much unlimited as limited. It is sovereign and unlimited in its disposition, its vocation, its possibilities and its historical purpose; it is not sovereign and it is limited in its individual expression and in its realisation at each particular moment."[1]

The Marxist doctrine about truth teaches us to avoid dogmatism, which lays down general principles, however arrived at, as unalterable and final truths—refusing to examine their foundations and refusing to alter and correct them, or if need be reject them altogether, in the light of new experience and new circumstances.

And at the same time it teaches us to avoid the narrow empiricism which confines itself to collecting and co-ordinating facts, is not interested in discovering the underlying laws of motion and interconnection manifested in those facts, and is sceptical about all bold generalisations and theories. Like dogmatism, empiricism cannot see beyond the limited experience of the present moment.

These attitudes, common enough in philosophy and the sciences, confront us also in the working class movement. In the working class movement dogmatism consists in learning certain formulas by rote and thinking that every new problem can be solved by simple repetition of these formulas. As a result of this, people fail to assimilate the lessons of experience and prove unable boldly to advance new policies to meet a new situation. Empiricism, on the other hand, consists in being engrossed in petty, day-to-day " practical " problems, attending only to these and regarding all other questions as unimportant, as the concern of " intellectuals " and not of practical workers. As a result of this, too, people fail to assimilate the lessons of experience and prove unable boldly to advance new policies. Thus both dogmatism and empiricism

[1] Engels, *loc. cit.*, Part I, ch. 9.

lead to the same result, and are capable of doing great harm to the working class movement, preventing it from finding the right road leading towards the achievement of socialism.

Marxism is both critical and revolutionary.

It is critical because it is against dogmas, insists on continual testing and re-testing of all ideas and all policies in the crucible of revolutionary practice—recognising that truth changes, that what is true enough today may become false tomorrow unless it is corrected and developed into new truth.

But simply to be critical is not enough. A merely critical attitude is negative and can lead to paralysis of action.

Marxism is also revolutionary. It is revolutionary because it does not only criticise, it goes forward to replace the old by the new. It is firm in its standpoint, certain of the truth and justice of its cause, confident in the correctness of its principles as the basis for the future advance, verifies its revolutionary ideas in revolutionary practice.

CHAPTER ELEVEN

THE ROOTS OF KNOWLEDGE

Knowledge is the sum of conceptions, views and propositions established and tested as correct reflections, so far as they go, of objective reality. It is essentially a social product, with its roots in social practice, tested and corrected by the fulfilment of expectations in practice. The beginning of all knowledge lies in sense perceptions, the reliability of which is proved in human practice. Knowledge can never be complete or final, but must always be expanded and criticised.

What is Knowledge?

IN achieving true ideas about things we also win and extend knowledge about them. What, then, is knowledge?

Unless we make our ideas correspond with reality, we certainly do not possess knowledge. To win knowledge is to replace ignorance or untrue ideas by true ideas. Hence the growth of knowledge is to be found in the growth of true ideas within the totality of ideas, some of which are true while others are not.

But simply to equate knowledge with truth is not to define knowledge. For the question arises: How do we *know* that our true ideas are true? Simply to state or believe something true is not to know it.

For example, some astronomers say there is life on Mars. Perhaps there is, in which case what they say is true. But they do not yet *know* there is life on Mars, for they have not yet gathered sufficient evidence. On the other hand, when astronomers say that Mars is a planet they are expressing knowledge of the matter; for in this case what they say is based on reliable methods of investigation.

Again, the ancient Greek philosophers said that bodies were composed of atoms. We today know that this is true—but they did not. It was simply a lucky guess on their part. How do we know that bodies are composed of atoms ? It is because while they merely speculated and made lucky guesses about the nature of matter, we have systematically investigated it, have based our ideas on such investigation, and so have tested and proved the truth of those particular ideas. On the other hand, there remain many things about which we know no more than the ancient Greeks—we are merely speculating about such things, just as they were ; and just as with them, it remains to be found out how near the truth are our speculations.

We gain knowledge, then, only in so far as we develop our ideas in such a way that their correspondence with reality is proved and tested. Only then can we lay claim to knowledge.

The development of knowledge is therefore the development of a special quality within the total development of our ideas, theories and views about things. Many ideas, theories and views about things have been worked out, often in the most systematic and logical way, but they have been merely speculative even if true, and have mostly been quite illusory. But in the course of the development of ideas there also occurs a development of knowledge, which is the development of ideas which not only correspond with reality but whose correspondence is proved and tested.

Our knowledge, then, is the sum of our conceptions, views and propositions which have been established and tested as correct reflections, so far as they go, of objective reality.

The Social Character of Knowledge

Knowledge is essentially a social product. It is built up socially, as a product of the social activity of men.

Some philosophers give both themselves and their readers a lot of trouble by trying to trace the growth of knowledge in the mind of the isolated individual and to find its roots in individual experience. In trying to do this, they set themselves an insoluble problem, since knowledge is not, and cannot be, built up in that way. An individual acting alone, cut off from contact with other people and relying only on himself, could acquire scarcely any knowledge at all—and that only of particular facts. Hence some of these philosophers were only following their own premises through to the logical conclusion when they announced that a man can know nothing except his own momentary existence, and certainly not the existence of the material world and of other people—though they were less logical in publishing this conclusion, since on their own showing they had no reason to believe that there existed anyone capable of reading it.

Of course, knowledge is built up by individuals—just as everything man creates is created by individuals; but it is built up by individuals acting in co-operation, depending on one another, communicating their experiences and their ideas. Many individuals in society can do what none of them individually could possibly do—and one of these things is to build up human knowledge. Every individual acquires a great deal of knowledge from his own experience; but he would not do so apart from his association with others, and if he did not learn from others what they had already learned. The very means for forming and expressing ideas, namely, language, without which no ideas would be possible, is a social product and exists only as the common possession of a society. Some individuals make especially great contributions to building up new knowledge, while many make no contribution at all; yet the former would not have made their contribution if they had not been members of a particular society, if they were not in communication with their fellows, if they had not learned what their society had to teach, if they had not had at their disposal the numerous material and intellectual means for acquiring knowledge which their society had produced.

It is, then, only in society that knowledge is acquired and built up, and its roots lie in the social activities of man. It is built up by the interchange of experiences and ideas between members of society in the course of their various forms of social activity, and it is sifted and tested in the same process.

As a result, the sum of social knowledge—that is, of

knowledge stored and available to society—is always greater than the knowledge possessed by individuals. Many people and many generations build up far more knowledge than any individual can possibly acquire. This knowledge is stored by society, being distributed in the first place amongst the many memories of many people, and secondly, being permanently recorded in writing—so that in this respect books and records of various kinds serve as a physical repository of the knowledge acquired in society. For instance, no one knows all the telephone numbers in London, but this knowledge is socially available and constantly made use of through the telephone directory. Again, no one knows everything discovered by the sciences, but the totality of this knowledge is socially available, and the organisation exists (though it could be greatly improved) for making use of it. So there exists in society an accumulation of social knowledge, to which individuals contribute and which individuals can draw upon.

Social Practice and Social Knowledge

All human association arises and develops from man's basic association in production. The development of knowledge, therefore, which is a product of human association, depends in the last analysis upon the development of social production. Men first began to form ideas in the process of production. And the development of thought and of knowledge, beginning in men's productive activity, can at no point be dissociated from it.

In the course of history knowledge has been won and consolidated step by step. And it is as men have striven to develop their forces of production, and to reconstitute their production relations corresponding to the development of their forces of production, that they have been impelled to strive for new knowledge and to overcome both the ignorance and false ideas which impeded their material progress.

" The Marxist regards man's productive activity as the most fundamental practical activity, as the determinant of all other activities," wrote Mao, in his exposition of the Marxist theory of knowledge. " In his cognition, man, depending mainly upon activity in material production, gradually understands nature's phenomena, nature's characteristics, nature's laws, and the relations between himself and nature ; and through productive activity he also gradually acquires knowledge in varying degrees about certain human institutions. None of such knowledge can be obtained apart from productive activity."[1]

The sum total of knowledge, and its character, at any stage of social development is, then, always dependent on and relative to the stage of development of production. For what men have been able to find out about nature and society always depends on their practical intercourse with nature and with one another, relates to the practical problems set by that inter-course, and is tested in the practical solution of those problems. On this basis they work out the categories of thought, modes of inference and methods of investigation by means of which the edifice of knowledge is built.

But while the development of knowledge depends in the last analysis on the development of production, it does not depend on production alone, but its development is mediated by the various forms of social activity and relationship which arise from production.

" Man's social practice is not confined to productive activity. There are many other forms of activity—class struggle, political life, scientific and artistic activity ; in short, man in society participates in all spheres of practical social life. Thus in his cognition, besides knowing things through his material produc-tive activity, man knows in varying degrees the various kinds of human inter-relations through political life and cultural life, both of which are closely connected with material life. Among these, the various forms of class struggle exert a particularly profound influence on the development of man's knowledge. In a class society everyone lives within the status of a particular class, and every mode of thought is invariably stamped with the brand of a class."[2]

The build-up of knowledge, then, dependent on material

[1] Mao Tse-tung, *On Practice.*
[2] *Ibid.*

productive activity, is also dependent, in class society, on classes and the class struggle. The task of preserving and enlarging the body of knowledge has in the main devolved upon the representatives of definite classes. And it has been largely as a result of the activity and struggle—economic, political, scientific and artistic—of different classes in different periods that new knowledge, both of nature and of society, has been won.

Theory and Practice in the Build-up of Knowledge

In general, the acquisition of knowledge in society is something which arises out of the sum total of the practical activities of the members of society, their intercourse with external nature and with one another. Apart from such practical activities, such active relationships, we could not acquire knowledge of anything, for there would be no basis on which to derive ideas which corresponded with objective reality or to test that correspondence.

Hence Lenin wrote : " The standpoint of life, of practice, should be first and fundamental in the theory of knowledge."[1]

What exactly do we mean by " practice " or " practical activity " ?

(1) First of all, practice consists of movements of the organs of the human body which cause changes in the surrounding world.

(2) But not simply any such movement, any such act, counts as practice or as practical activity. For instance, we would not count various simple reflex actions as examples of practice. Nor would we give the title of practical activity to the actions of a sleepwalker. Practical activity is essentially human conscious activity ; that is to say, it is done deliberately, with (a) an idea of the end result, or aim, to be achieved, and (b) some consciousness of the conditions of the action and of the properties of the subject of the action and of the means through which the aim can be achieved.

(3) Thirdly, practice is social. There is, of course, individual

[1] Lenin, *Materialism and Empirio-Criticism*, ch. 2, section 6.

practice—that is, the practical activities carried out by an individual on his own—and also social practice, activities which can be carried out only by a number of individuals acting in association. But no conscious practical activity would develop apart from man's social life and the conditioning of individuals by their society.

In society, people develop many means to their practical activity. Speech, by which we communicate with one another, is one of them. Hence a large and important part is played in our practical activity by speech, for this is certainly an important means of bringing things about.

The above three points define what we mean by " practice ".

Knowledge, then, arises out of practice because it arises out of the development of ideas corresponding to the various conditions, subjects and means of our practical activities. Practice demands such ideas, and they are developed in accordance with the development of practice. Knowledge is acquired just in so far as practice creates the demand for true ideas about various things, and provides the means and opportunities for working them out and testing them.

At all times it has been social practice which has impelled people to develop and perfect their knowledge—the requirements of the development of material productive activity, and no less the requirements of the different classes, who have experienced the necessity of acquiring ever deeper knowledge about various aspects of nature and society in order to carry forward their own practical interests.

Thus as men have improved their instruments of production, their production technique, their practical ability to master nature, so has their knowledge of nature advanced. For changes in production set problems for knowledge and at the same time provide the means for tackling them. New fields of knowledge are thus opened up, and new and far-reaching conclusions reached. These in turn contribute to further technical advance and are tested, and also further developed, in their application in practice.

The capitalist class, in undertaking the development of

modern industry, gave a profound impulse to the deepening of natural knowledge, particularly of physical and chemical processes. The working class in turn, in undertaking and leading the building of socialism, requires and creates the conditions for far more comprehensive natural knowledge.

Similarly, as men have striven to improve their well-being and have succeeded in establishing new and higher social relations in place of old and outmoded ones, so has their knowledge of themselves and of society advanced.

The knowledge of the laws of social change embodied in scientific socialism could be achieved only when, with the development of the working class, the struggle for socialism became a practical question. In general, in each historical epoch the extent of knowledge of society and its laws has always corresponded to the practical social tasks of the epoch. Thus capitalism, by the development of the world market and then the division of the world among imperialist powers, stimulated studies in world history and in societies at various stages of their development, which resulted in a tremendous enlargement of social and historical research. Going beyond this, the struggle for socialism laid the basis for truly scientific knowledge of society, penetrating to the basic social relationships and laws of social development.

On the other hand, people do not and cannot acquire knowledge of things about which their practice has not yet given them the need or opportunity of finding out anything. For example, while people still lived in small local communes and used very primitive instruments of production they did not and could not develop any knowledge of geography, or of mathematics, or astronomy, or mechanics. They knew very little, though they had all sorts of ideas about things of which they knew little. Before capitalism and the emergence of the working class people did not and could not acquire much knowledge about the laws of development of society and the inevitability of socialism. They had all sorts of ideas about such things, including ideas of socialism, but very little knowledge.

Knowledge, which arises out of practice, is tested in practice.

For the correspondence of our ideas about the conditions, subjects and means of practical activity with the objective reality independent of our ideas is tested, and can in the last resort only be tested, by the results of the activity which is guided by those ideas.

Every act is done with certain expectations, which are based on the ideas which guide the act. The only final test of the correspondence of ideas with reality lies in the fulfilment or non-fulfilment of the expectations based on ideas.

If, on the other hand, we have ideas which are in no way related to expectations of the results of practice, and which therefore cannot be tested by reference to the fulfilment or non-fulfilment of expectations, then there is no way of ever deciding the correspondence or non-correspondence of such ideas with reality—in other words, they can form no part of knowledge, but are merely illusory or speculative.

So Marx wrote: " The question whether objective truth can be attributed to human thinking is not a question of theory but is a practical question. In practice man must prove the truth, i.e., the reality and power, the ' this-sidedness ' of his thinking. The dispute over the reality or non-reality [that is, the correspondence or non-correspondence with reality—M.C.] of thinking which is isolated from practice is a purely scholastic question."[1]

We gain knowledge, then, by working out ideas arising out of problems of practice, and we step by step test our knowledge, in other words, establish it as knowledge, by reference to the fulfilment or non-fulfilment of our expectations in practice.

Hence knowledge in its development continually passes through a cycle of three phases :

(1) Social practice, the development of production and of social relationships, setting problems for theoretical solution.

(2) The elaboration of theories arising from those problems, based on the available experiences, and the logical working out of those theories.

(3) The application of those theories in social practice,

[1] Marx, *Theses on Feuerbach*, II.

testing, verifying and correcting them in the process of putting them to use.

This is a never-ending process. For whatever may be our knowledge, new demands of practice lead to new extensions of knowledge. Moreover, existing knowledge must always be brought into conformity with the lessons and demands of practice. Hence as new knowledge is won, old theories are reformulated, existing knowledge is both corrected and deepened.

So summing up the teachings of the dialectical materialist theory of knowledge, Mao Tse-tung wrote :

" The Marxist holds that man's social practice alone is the criterion of the truth of his knowledge of the external world. In reality, man's knowledge becomes verified only when, in the process of social practice (in the process of material production, of class struggle, and of scientific experiment) he achieves the anticipated results. . . . The theory of knowledge of dialectical materialism raises practice to the first place, holds that human knowledge cannot be separated in the least bit from practice, and repudiates all theories which deny the importance of practice or separate knowledge from practice. . . .

" Practice, knowledge, more practice, more knowledge ; the cyclical repetition of this pattern to infinity, and with each cycle the elevation of the content of practice and knowledge to a higher level. Such is the dialectical materialist theory of knowledge, and such is the dialectical materialist theory of the unity of knowing and doing."[1]

Sense-Perception, the Beginning of All Knowledge

In this whole process of acquiring and building knowledge, on what do we have to rely in obtaining information about things, and in carrying out the test of the fulfilment or non-fulfilment of expectations ? We have to rely on our senses.

Separating knowledge from practice, many philosophers have also maintained that knowledge is built up by a process of " pure thought ". The senses, they say, are unreliable, and

[1] Mao Tse-tung, *loc. cit.*

cannot be a source of knowledge, to gain which we should ignore the data of sense and rely on the intellect alone.

Yet human knowledge, capable as it is of indefinite expansion, is always the work of the human brain. The brain is the organ of the most complicated relations of man with the external world, and in elaborating these relationships we are dependent, in the first place, on the signals received through the senses as a result of our interaction with the things outside us. The beginning of all our knowledge, then, can be nothing else than the sense perceptions we acquire in the course of life activity. Knowledge can be built on no other basis than the information gained through the exercise of our senses, through sense perceptions which have their source in the objective material world. " For the person who shuts his eyes, stops his ears and totally cuts himself off from the objective world, there can be no knowledge to speak of. Knowledge starts with experience. This is the materialism of the theory of knowledge".[1]

This materialist point of view in the theory of knowledge was embodied in Lenin's well known definition of matter, as " the objective reality which is given to man by his sensations, and which is reflected by our sensations while existing independently of them".[2] This emphasises that the material world is the world accessible to the senses. What we know about the material world is derived from the exercise of our senses. Any supposed knowledge which goes beyond that is not knowledge but fantasy, and any supposed objective reality inaccessible to the senses is not real but imaginary.

It may be objected that these are dogmatic statements. But there is no dogma here. On the contrary, once we get away from this fundamental materialist position we get away from all verifiable knowledge and into the realms of pure speculation. Once we allow ourselves to start inventing " realities " which cannot in any way be detected by the instrumentality of the senses, we are away into the clouds. We are faced with the sort of questions the later scholastics used to ask : " How many

[1] *Ibid.*
[2] Lenin, *Materialism and Empirio-Criticism*, ch. 2, section 4.

angels can stand on the point of a needle ? " There is no possible way of detecting them, and so of checking the answer to the question. That is why we can be sure that such questions and such speculations have nothing whatever to do with knowledge, and are simply ways of bamboozling people.

Indeed, to say we gain knowledge only through the exercise of the senses in the course of practical activity is no more a dogma than to say we cannot live without eating. To promise people " supersensible " or " transcendent " knowledge is like promising them the means of eternal life while offering them nothing to eat—and the promises are often made by the same learned and pious people. The materialist theory of knowledge is a defence and weapon against such deceptions.

Hence we should steadily reject all " principles " and dogmas which claim to be known independent of experience, independent of the exercise of the senses, whether by some inner light or by virtue of some authority. We should not trust those who seek to impose their views because they claim to possess some special intellectual gift, or to have been initiated into some mystery, or to be empowered with some special authority. We should be sceptical, and accept nothing from anyone which cannot be explained and justified in terms of practice and sense experience. For we cannot know of the existence or properties of anything except in so far as its existence and properties are capable of being detected, in some way, directly or indirectly, by our senses.

The Reliability of the Senses

But can we trust our senses ? How do we know that our senses do not always deceive us, as they sometimes do in hallucinations and dreams ? More generally, how do we know that anything at all exists corresponding to our perceptions ?

To answer these questions we must remember that we acquire and build up our perceptions of objects only in the course of practical activity. The information which we gain through the senses does not just come to us. We get it in practical life, by conscious, practical interaction with the objects outside us.

A new-born baby, for example, starts with a mass of confused impressions of itself and the outside world. It begins to use its senses and to get information about the objects which surround it when it begins to reach out for those objects, to see what it can do with them, to investigate them, to experiment with and test them in all sorts of ways.

Just as each member of the human race starts getting information about the world in that way, so that is the way in which all knowledge about the world is acquired and built up. Our first confused impressions of an unfamiliar thing are certainly not reliable and provide little if any information about it. We use our senses to obtain information about it by investigating it. And we continually test the reliability of our perceptions of it in the course of our practical dealings with it.

Apart from such practical dealings with things outside us, we have no way of telling whether our perceptions agree with objects or, indeed, whether any object at all corresponds to them. But when we act on our perceptions, and when we turn things to our own use according to the qualities we perceive in them, then we test whether or not, and how far, our perceptions agree with reality outside ourselves.

A philosopher sitting alone in his study and trying to conjure up knowledge from the inner resources of his own mind may make great difficulty about this. He wonders whether his study, his books, the chair he is sitting on, and his own body sitting on it, really exist, or whether they are some kind of dream or illusion in his mind. But outside his study, outside the academic discussions of philosophers, there is no difficulty.

" Human action had solved the difficulty long before human ingenuity invented it ", wrote Engels. " The proof of the pudding is in the eating. From the moment we turn to our own use these objects according to the qualities we perceive in them, we put to an infallible test the correctness or otherwise of our sense perceptions. If these perceptions have been wrong, then our estimate of the use to which an object can be turned must also be wrong, and our attempt must fail. But if we succeed in accomplishing our aim, if we find that the object does agree with our idea of it, and does answer the purpose we intended for it, then that is positive proof that our perceptions of it and of its qualities, so far, agree with reality outside ourselves. . . . So long as we take care to train and use our senses properly, and to keep our action within the limits prescribed by perceptions properly made and properly used, so long we shall find that the result of our action proves the conformity of our perceptions with the objective nature of the things perceived."[1]

The material world exists, and we are part of it. We learn about the bodies outside us and about the state of our own bodies by our senses. So naturally we have no other way of finding out about the world—that is, of gaining knowledge— than through the exercise of our senses. Nor can our senses be so constituted as always or even usually to deceive us. If they were, we would not be able to live at all.

" The products of the human brain," wrote Engels, " being in the last analysis also products of nature, do not contradict the rest of nature but are in correspondence with it."[2] Our senses are necessarily so constituted as to provide us with perceptions which agree with reality outside ourselves. These perceptions, which are the beginning of all our knowledge, are gained in the course of practical activity, and their agreement with reality is brought about and tested in practical activity.

So all our knowledge—that is to say, the sum of our conceptions which are established and tested as correct reflections so far as they go, of objective reality—is established on the basis of the perceptions we gain in our practical activity, and is likewise tested in the same activity.

The Expansion, Incompleteness and Criticism of Knowledge

Some philosophers have believed that the goal of knowledge is to attain a complete, rounded-off system, encompassing knowledge of everything that exists to be known. And a few have believed that they themselves had actually attained such a

[1] Engels, *Socialism, Utopian and Scientific*, Introduction.
[2] Engels, *Anti-Duhring*, Part I, ch. 3.

goal—as was alleged of the late Master of Balliol, Professor B. Jowett :

> Here I stand, my name is Jowett,
> There's no knowledge but I know it.
> I am Master of this College,
> And what I don't know isn't knowledge.

Yet neither as a whole nor in any of its various departments can human knowledge ever be finished, finalised and rounded-off. Knowledge is always growing and developing. Indeed, this is obvious when we consider that our knowledge all arises from and is tested in practice, and is derived from the sense perceptions we gain in practical activity. We shall never have done everything that can be done, or have examined every aspect of everything that ever existed, exists or will exist. There will always be more to do, more to find out in doing it, and therefore more to know.

So knowledge is always expanding, or, at least, capable of expansion ; and therefore always incomplete. And there are two aspects of this expansion and incompleteness of knowledge.

The first aspect is a quantitative one. New knowledge is always being added to old knowledge, so that we come to know more. And this expansion takes place in two dimensions, so to speak—in breadth and depth of knowledge. We get to know about new things which we did not know about before ; and we get to know more about the things concerning which we already knew something. In this way we can always know more, but never know all.

For example, in modern physics we have got to know about " fundamental particles " the existence of which was not previously known ; and in getting to know about them, we have also increased or deepened our knowledge about atoms and their structure, concerning which something was already known. But because we have in this way increased the breadth and depth of our physical knowledge, we cannot conclude that we have completed our physical knowledge. On the contrary, all we should conclude is that while we have more physical knowledge than our predecessors, our successors, starting where we leave off, will have more still.

The second aspect is a qualitative one. When we get to know more, the addition of this more to what we already knew does not leave what we already knew unaffected. On the contrary, knowledge of new things and more knowledge of old things throws a new light, so to speak, on what we already knew. As a result, we can find new implications and new significance in what we had already established; and at the same time we find that, in the light of the new knowledge, certain implications drawn from the old were wrong, and it must be reconsidered and reformulated in various ways.

For example, new discoveries in physics which were summed up in quantum mechanics cast a new light on the older discoveries in physics which were summed up in classical mechanics. As a result, the old knowledge had to be reconsidered and reformulated in various ways, and it became clear that some of the conclusions drawn from it were wrong. Again, when in the practice of building socialism in one country, the Soviet Union, new knowledge was gained about the nature and functions of the socialist state, it became necessary to reconsider and reformulate some of the propositions about the socialist state previously put forward by Marxism, and it became clear that some of the conclusions drawn from it were wrong.

None of this means that old knowledge turns out to have been illusory and so not to have been real knowledge at all. All it means is that the incompleteness of old knowledge leads to the necessity of its being critically reformulated in the light of new knowledge. And the same will apply, of course, to the new knowledge itself, when it in turn becomes old knowledge.

So " the history of human knowledge tells us ", wrote Mao Tse-tung, " that the truth of many theories is incomplete and that this incompleteness is remedied only through the test of practice. . . . Generally speaking, whether in the practice of changing nature or of changing society, people's original ideas, theories, plans or programmes are seldom realised without any change whatever."[1]

Knowledge grows through a process of not only adding to

[1] Mao Tse-tung, *loc. cit.*

but also perfecting and correcting the already existing body of knowledge. In no field is knowledge ever perfect, final and complete. Consequently, whatever knowledge has been established must be accepted only as a point of departure for further advances of knowledge—just as whatever has been achieved in practice should not be regarded as a final achievement but only as a point of departure for further gains. This means that we must also be prepared to recognise that all knowledge is always limited, incomplete, defective, and so requires not only supplementation but also criticism in order to carry it forward and advance to new conquests.

CHAPTER TWELVE

THE GROWTH OF KNOWLEDGE

Knowledge is acquired and grows in the process of our entering into active relations with things, in which we pass from perceptions to judgments. The growth of knowledge takes place through the passage from perceptual to rational knowledge, from merely superficial judgments about the appearances of things to reasoned conclusions about their essential properties, interconnections and laws. In this way we acquire ever more profound knowledge of the objective world. At every stage our knowledge is limited, but it advances by overcoming these limits.

From Ignorance to Knowledge

THE acquisition of knowledge, and the build-up of knowledge, is by its very nature always a process of the passage from ignorance to knowledge, from not knowing things to knowing them. Whether we consider our knowledge in general, or our knowledge of some particular thing, it is always the case that first we knew nothing and then gradually acquired knowledge.

Hence Lenin wrote that the theory of knowledge must study " the transition from *non*-knowledge to knowledge".[1] " We must not regard our knowledge as ready made," he wrote, " . . . but must determine how knowledge emerges from ignorance, how incomplete, inexact knowledge becomes more complete and more exact."[2]

Many philosophers, on the other hand, have taken it for granted that knowledge can only be derived from previous knowledge. Therefore they have supposed that there must be fundamental certainties, from which all knowledge is derived.

[1] Lenin, *Karl Marx*.
[2] Lenin, *Materialism and Empirio-Criticism*, ch. 2, section 1.

This leads them to two opposite but equally misleading conclusions. On the one hand, they invent various principles which they say are certain, and then claim that they know and have proved all the propositions deduced from these principles. On the other hand, they deny a great part of our real knowledge, because it cannot be so deduced. Thus, for example, philosophers have deduced all manner of conclusions about God and the ultimate nature of reality from first principles; and on the other hand, they have rejected the whole of our knowledge about the material world on the grounds that it cannot be justified by anything they are prepared to accept as absolutely certain and self-evident.

Yet the real starting point of knowledge is not knowledge but ignorance, and not certainty but uncertainty. We always build up knowledge from a previous state of lack of knowledge. Hence to try to build up systems of knowledge from self-evident premises is to misunderstand the whole problem of building knowledge, and must always be in vain.

How, then, is knowledge built up from ignorance? This is done, and can only be done, through our sensuous interaction with things. It is done by human brains, which, as we have repeatedly said, are the organs of the most complicated relations between man and the external world. By the perceptual awareness of things which results from entering into various active relations with them, we come to know them where previously we did not know them. And the more various the relations with things into which we enter, the more do we consequently get to know about them. Hence knowledge is the product of our consciously entering into active relations with things. The transition from lack of knowledge to knowledge is wrought by human activity passing from lack of relation with things to relation with things.

For instance, we did not know the source of the Nile; we got to know it by going there. We did not know the composition of atoms; we got to know it by performing experiments. We did not know the distances of the stars; we got to know by devising methods of measuring them. We did not know the laws of development of human society; we got to know by consciously striving to utilise them for bringing about a new stage of social development.

Perceptions and Judgments

The first requisite for the build-up of knowledge is obtaining perceptions—that is, making observations arising out of various relationships with things. First we had no observations relative to some thing or process, then we obtained such observations : this is the first step. Without performing it, there can only be ignorance, not knowledge—either blank ignorance or else, as often happens, ignorance camouflaged by illusory or speculative theories about things.

Secondly, having entered into relationship with things and obtained observations about them, we must go on to formulate judgments or propositions about them and their properties and relations. We must employ the laws of thought—that is, the logical laws for the reflection of objective reality in terms of ideas—in order to express in ideas, in judgments or propositions the results of observations.

The build-up of knowledge always involves the passage from perceptions to ideas. All the higher animals have perceptions, and in their perceptions possess definite, concrete information about things, which they learn to make more reliable and which they use in their life activity. But only in man is this information provided by the senses converted into knowledge, in the sense of being expressed in ideas and propositions.

Here we understand the term " knowledge " in the definite sense of *human* knowledge. The sense in which, for example, a dog knows the way home is different from the sense in which a man knows the way, for in the latter case it is expressible in ideas and propositions which can be communicated. Ideas and propositions are communicated, shared and discussed by people in their social life, and it is this expression of information in ideas and propositions which constitutes the essential feature of human knowledge. People acquire and possess knowledge just in so far as they pass from the perceptions which are particular to each individual and which they possess in common with all animals, to the ideas, judgments, propositions which are socially communicated and are peculiar to man—in other words, from the utilisation of the concrete signals of the first signal system which man possesses in common with the animals to the second signal system which is specific to the human being.

Perception by itself, then, is only the condition of knowledge, but not as yet its realisation. The knowledge of things possessed by man is achieved by passing from perceptions of them to judgments founded on perceptions.

Thus in the cycle, which we noted in the last chapter, of " practice, knowledge, more practice, more knowledge ", knowledge is always being built up by a continual cycle of qualitatively distinct activities which together make up the whole process of knowing—entering into active relationships with things ; obtaining from this relationship perceptions and observations ; formulating judgments out of the observations ; utilising these judgments to direct the further active relationships with things, leading to further observations, further judgments, and so on without end.

From Superficial to More Profound Judgments

Sense perception reproduces things as they immediately appear through their action on our sense organs. The senses give only particular pieces of information about particular things conditioned by the particular circumstances under which we are perceiving them.

By expressing the information obtained from perception in propositions people arrive at judgments expressing conclusions from the comparison and putting together of many particular data of perception. " The first step in the process of knowledge ", wrote Mao Tse-tung, " is contact with the things of the external world ; this belongs to the stage of perception. The second step is a synthesis of the data of perception by making a rearrangement or reconstruction ; this belongs to the stage of conception, judgment and inference."[1]

[1] Mao Tse-tung, *On Practice.*

For example, from many perceptions of many members of society we reach such conclusions (all of which represent elementary items of social knowledge) as " dogs bark ", " cows give milk ", " water turns into ice in cold weather ", and so on. Such judgments are, as Mao expressed it, " a synthesis of the data of perception ".

To form such judgments about things depends not on a single observation by a single person but on several or many observations by several or many people. And the more various the observations, the more various the circumstances in which and the angles from which they are made, and the more various the changes and relationships of the object which they cover, the more comprehensively and faithfully can the judgment reflect the objective properties, relations and forms of motion of the object.

Observation is itself an activity, since we must consciously bring ourselves into relation with something if we are to observe it, and must bring ourselves into more varied relation—noting various different aspects of the thing, its various changes, and so on—if we are to observe it more fully. But observation itself passes from what may be called passive observation to active observation, and it is the latter which is of primary importance for building up fuller knowledge of things.

Observation in itself does not change that which is observed. In this sense, it is passive. A bird-watcher, for example, obtains knowledge about birds, but he does not interfere with them in any way in making his observations ; on the contrary, in this case he must be very careful not to do so. Active observation arises when we ourselves, by our activity, take a part in bringing the things which we observe into new relationships or bringing about various changes in them, and observe the results of the relationships or changes which we ourselves have effected under our own control.

One of the most important methods of active observation of things is, for example, to measure them. The process of measurement, whatever it may be we are measuring, involves bringing one thing into relationship with another thing and noting the results. Other methods of active observation are, for example, to break something down into its parts or elements and then to reconstitute it again, or to effect changes in its properties through the agency of other things. In general, by elaborating methods of active observation suitable to the different things we want to know about and what we want to know about them, we obtain many significant observations, leading us to conclusions about their properties, relations, motions, laws of motion, causes and effects, composition, and so on.

Having acquired, through both passive and active observations and their translation into judgments, a certain body of knowledge expressed in judgments, we can then make use of this knowledge in order to obtain more knowledge. For it will suggest new fields of exploration and methods for establishing new relationships with things. Knowledge already built up is utilised for the direction of more activity and the obtaining out of it of more observations. By this means, the knowledge already built up is further tested and corrected, and the whole build-up of knowledge is continued.

The process of passing from observation to judgment, and then from more active and comprehensive observation to more comprehensive judgment, brings about, in the first place, a correction of immediate conclusions based on insufficient observation.

Ordinary experience already teaches us that there is a difference between the first appearance of things in sense-perception and their reality. For it often happens that things turn out to be different from what they at first appear to be, and this is shown in practice by the non-realisation of expectations based on first appearances. In the process of building up knowledge we are always passing from conclusions which express only the apparent properties, relations and motions of things to conclusions which approximate more fully to things as they really are.

For example, when we perceive the sun it looks a relatively small body—and for a long time people concluded that it was in fact quite small. But we have come to know that the sun is in fact very big. Again, the sun looks as if it goes round the earth—and for a long time people concluded that it did in fact go round the earth. But we have come to know that it is the earth which really goes round the sun.

In the second place, in the process of forming more comprehensive judgments about things we pass from fragmentary knowledge of particular things, with their particular properties, relations and motions, to more connected knowledge of their laws of existence, change and interconnections.

The first knowledge which is based on the first observations of things is knowledge of a number of facts about those things, but not of the laws of their existence and the interconnections between them which manifest themselves in and determine those facts. At the same time, therefore, as we correct the conclusions based on the first appearance of things and form judgments about their real properties, relations and motions which give rise to the appearances, we also form judgments about the general laws and interconnections which are manifested in the particular properties, motions and relations of things first evident to observation.

For example, having established the main facts about the solar system—that the planets, of which the earth is one, go round the sun—we also establish the laws which are manifested in the system and by the operation of which it exists and remains in being.

Again, knowing from common experience that water turns into ice when it grows cold enough, we go on to establish—as a result of the synthesis of, and inferences drawn from, many special observations—the reasons for this phenomenon, namely, that it is due to a rearrangement of the molecules caused by changes in their motion when the temperature is lowered.

Thus in the process of passing from observation to judgment we also succeed in passing from superficial to more profound judgments—from judgments which simply state what we have observed to judgments which go further, and draw conclusions about the composition and internal organisation of things, about their causes and effects, interactions, interconnections and motions, and laws of interconnection and motion.

This is a qualitative change in the content of judgments; a passage from judgments of superficial content to judgments of a more profound content; from judgments in terms of elementary ideas to which correspond objects directly perceptible to the senses, to judgments in terms of abstract ideas, which state the causes, reasons, explanations, consequences, laws of the things we observe.[1]

From Perceptual to Rational Knowledge

We can conclude that knowledge in general is realised only by passing from perception to judgment, and that then the process of developing the knowledge expressed in judgments, of extending and deepening it, passes through two qualitatively distinct stages—first, the superficial and fragmentary knowledge of things directly derived from perceptions of them; and second, knowledge of their essential properties, interconnections and laws.

In the first stage, our judgments express merely " the separate aspects of things, the external relations between such things". In the second stage, we arrive at judgments which " no longer represent the appearances of things, their separate aspects, or their external relations, but embrace their essence, their totality and their internal relations".[2]

The passage from the first stage to the second stage involves, in the first place, active observation. Without active observation, the data on which to found more profound and comprehensive judgments will be lacking, and any judgments which may be made can only be speculative or illusory.

In the second place, however, it involves a process of thought arising from observation—a process of the sifting and comparison of observations, of generalisation and formation of abstract ideas, of reasoning and drawing conclusions from such

[1] This is the passage which Hegel was the first to begin to analyse scientifically in his great book *The Science of Logic*, and which he called the passage from the categories of " Being " to the categories of " Essence ".

[2] Mao Tse-tung, *loc. cit.*

generalisation and abstraction. Having reached conclusions, they must be again checked with active observation, in order to ensure that they accord with it and that the abstract generalisations reached by thought do express the concrete facts given in perception. The passage from the first stage to the second stage therefore involves a passage from judgments which directly express the data of perception, to judgments which are derived from the data of perception through a process of abstraction and generalisation.

The passage from the judgment that the sun is hot to the judgment that its surface temperature is about 6,000 degrees Centigrade represents, for example, such a passage of knowledge from the first to the second stage. The judgment that the sun is hot directly expresses one way in which the sun affects our senses. But the judgment about its temperature involves, first, that we have formed the abstract idea of temperature, and second, that with the aid of this idea we have reached conclusions about the sun's temperature by an elaborate process of active observation and reasoning based on it.   As a result we pass from a judgment which merely expresses certain observations about the sun, to one which expresses its internal state.

Again, suppose that we are considering the state organisation of a given country, of Great Britain let us say. The first observations which may be made concern particular facts—such as that the capital is London, that laws are made by people sitting in two Houses of Parliament, that these laws are signed by the Queen and enforced by policemen, and so on. Many inquiries into the character of British parliamentary democracy never get further than formulating the judgments summarising such observations, which means that they go no further than the first stage of knowledge. If, however, inquiry is carried further, if the state is considered in its historical development on the basis of the whole development of the economic structure of society, and if reasoned conclusions are drawn from this inquiry, then we will arrive at the judgment that the British parliamentary state is the organ of rule of the

British capitalist class. This is to advance knowledge of the state to the second stage, which embraces not merely a number of observed facts about it but its essential nature.

In his work on the theory of knowledge, Mao Tse-tung called the first stage of knowledge " perceptual knowledge ", because it confines itself to summarising observations, and the second stage " rational knowledge ", or " logical knowledge ", because it is reached by a process of abstraction and reasoning employing the laws of logic.

" The reason why logical knowledge is different from perceptual knowledge ", he wrote, " is that perceptual knowledge concerns the separate aspects of things, the appearances, the external relations of things ; whereas logical knowledge takes a big stride forward to reach the wholeness, the essence and the internal relations of things, discloses the internal contradictions of the surrounding world, and is therefore capable of grasping the development of the surrounding world in its totality, in the internal relations between all its aspects."[1]

Many philosophers (those belonging to the so-called " empiricist " and " positivist " schools) have denied that knowledge develops through two such stages. According to them, first we obtain various " sense data ", and then we compare and relate these data in order to formulate judgments or propositions summarising the observations. And for them, that is the whole process of knowledge. Hence, for them, knowledge is entirely confined to " the separate aspects of things, the appearances, the external relations of things ", and it is an illusion to suppose that there can be any more profound knowledge of things—of their essence as opposed to their appearance to us, of their essential properties, interconnections and laws.

In opposition to this empiricist or positivist type of philosophy, Marxism traces the growth of knowledge from a lower to a higher stage. First of all, in obtaining information through the senses we pass from sensations to perceptions, that is, from separate signals of the various senses to the co-ordination

[1] *Ibid.*

of signals in perceptions ; and then, in the development of our knowledge expressed in ideas and judgments, we pass from perceptual knowledge of the appearances and external relations of things to rational knowledge of their essential characteristics and internal relations.

Appearance and Essence

In passing from elementary to abstract ideas, from superficial to more profound judgments, from perceptual to rational knowledge, the passage is made from the appearance of things to their essence. In considering knowledge, a distinction must always be made between appearance and essence—between the particular phenomena which are immediately evident to observation and the essential characteristics, interconnections and laws which are manifested in the appearances and underlie the observed facts. The task of knowing things is always to advance from appearance to essence, so as to grasp their essential nature which is manifested in their particular existence and mode of appearance, to grasp their essential interconnections and laws.

Thus Marx stressed that the task of science is always to proceed from the immediate knowledge of appearances to the discovery of the essence, the essential connections and laws, underlying the appearances, and so finally to reach a comprehensive understanding of the appearances.

Inquiry, he wrote, " has to appropriate the material in detail, to analyse its different forms of development, to trace out their inner connections. Only after this work is done can the actual movement be adequately described. If this is done successfully . . . the life of the subject matter is ideally reflected as in a mirror."[1]

So Marx stressed that knowledge of the essential character and laws of any subject-matter must always be derived from a detailed analysis of all the relevant facts, and must in turn serve to explain them—to demonstrate their inner connections and actual movement.

His own work in the social sciences provides examples of

[1] Marx, *Capital*, Preface to 2nd edition.

this point. Thus in *Capital* Marx pointed out that whereas the " vulgar economists " dealt only with the surface appearances of capitalist economy, scientific political economy seeks to uncover the real relations of production underlying the appearances, and on that basis explain the appearances. If the underlying essential connections had been evident on the surface to superficial observation, there would have been no need for further profound inquiry. But the essence of things is never evident on the surface, and can be discovered only by painstaking scientific analysis.

" The way of thinking of the vulgar economists ", wrote Marx, " derives from the fact that it is always only the immediate form in which relationships appear which is reflected in the brain, and not their inner connections. If the latter were the case, moreover, what would be the need for a science at all ? " And explaining his own method of scientific analysis of capitalist economy, he pointed out that at the end of it, " we have arrived at the forms of appearance which serve as the starting point for the vulgar : ground rent coming from the earth, profit (interest) from capital, and wages from labour. But from our point of view the thing is now seen differently. The apparent movement is explained."[1]

It is clear from this, incidentally, that the positivist philosophy, which confines knowledge entirely to dealing with surface appearances, was completely in accord with the procedures of the " vulgar economists " whom Marx criticised, and their procedures were completely in accord with it. This philosophy, indeed, is the most suitable philosophy for the apologists of capitalism, whose whole outlook depends on their never looking below the surface of social life.

As a vivid example of the importance of judging things, not from superficial appearances but from the point of view of their inner relationships and connections, we could take the case of wages. If we judge only from external appearances, then wages are simply payment for work. A man works so many hours and is paid so much per hour. In that case, we

[1] Marx, *Letters* to Engels, June 27, 1867, and April 30, 1858.

could perceive no difference between wages in, say, capitalist society and in socialist society. Whether he works in a capitalist or a socialist factory, a man works so many hours and gets paid so much. What is the difference? The difference is that the external form of wages expresses different social relations. In capitalist society, wages are the price of the worker's labour-power, which he has sold to the capitalist. In socialist society, wages are no longer the price of labour-power, since the factories belong to the working people, who do not sell their labour-power to themselves. Wages now express the allocation to the worker of a definite share of the values he has produced according to the work he has contributed. So while in capitalist society the workers can maintain or raise their wages only by fighting the capitalist class and threatening to strike, in socialist society they continually raise their standards by increasing production. In other words, the laws which determine wages are totally different in socialist from capitalist society. But why they are different can only be understood when we go behind the appearances of things and seek to discover the inner relationships and connections which determine the appearances.

Revolutionary Theory and Revolutionary Practice

To pass from superficial to profound judgment about things, and from their appearance to their essence, is, as we have said, to pass from one stage of knowing things to another. Such a qualitative change in knowledge is also as a rule a revolutionary change. It is revolutionary because it brings about a revolutionary change in what we can do.

When practice is guided only by what we have learned concerning the external appearance of things, then it lacks the power of knowingly bringing about profound changes in those things, or of utilising them extensively for far-reaching purposes. On the contrary, when we know things only by their appearances we generally have in practice to wait on what happens, to adapt ourselves to things—often badly and suffering surprises, set-backs and misfortunes—rather than mastering them and adapting them to purposes of our own.

But when we begin to grasp the essence of something, then we can deal with it more effectively, bring about profound changes in it and utilise it for our own purposes.

For example, up to modern times people had only superficial knowledge of chemical processes, and so there could be little effectively planned use of these processes in production. But modern chemistry enables us to break substances down and bring them into being again from their constituents, so that many materials can be made by synthetic methods, with properties to suit our own requirements. We can split atoms, break down one element into others and utilise the energy produced in the process, and even create new man-made elements, such as plutonium.

Again, the utopian socialists and the old working class movement could not effectively change society. But Marxist theory, which penetrates to the essence of social processes, has enabled the working class movement thoroughly to transform society in some countries and to begin to build socialism.

Whether we consider knowledge of nature or of society, whenever knowledge has been raised to knowledge of the essence of a subject then this has been a revolutionary development, a revolution in what people can do.

Such profound advances in knowledge—whether they have been consciously linked with practice or not by those who played the major theoretical part in effecting them—are always in the last analysis the products of revolutionary strivings in social practice. It is when people strive to do something new so as to increase their powers and improve their conditions, that they experience the necessity of raising their knowledge to knowledge of the essence of some subject. There can be no revolutionary practice without knowledge, for without knowledge it lacks direction and cannot attain its goal. A leap forward in knowledge is a condition for the realisation of a revolution in practice.

In the sphere of knowledge, it is impossible to raise the knowledge of things to the level of rational knowledge apart from or in advance of the corresponding practice, just as practice gropes in the dark without the necessary knowledge. Apart from the appropriate practice no genuine knowledge is possible, but only guesswork and speculation. All genuine knowledge arises out of practice, and in turn is tested in practice—though this does not mean that the theoretical deductions from a discovery may not advance beyond the carrying into effect of all its potential practical consequences. There is no other way to discover the essential interconnections and laws of the real world than the way of entering into practical relations with real objects and processes, striving to master and change them, forming concepts on the basis of the experiences gained, and then testing the theoretical conclusions once more in living practice.

Like all knowledge, therefore, knowledge about the essence of things is also tested only by practice. Revolutionary knowledge is tested by revolutionary practice, by the very success with which revolutionary practice utilises the discovery made in the sphere of knowledge. And the knowledge itself is consolidated, further developed, criticised and corrected in this process.

" Knowledge starts with practice, reaches the theoretical plane via practice, and then has to return to practice. The active function of knowledge not only manifests itself in the active leap from perceptual knowledge to rational knowledge, but also—and this is the more important—in the leap from rational knowledge to revolutionary practice. The knowledge which enables us to grasp the laws of the world must be re-directed to the practice of changing the world—that is, it must again be applied in the practice of production, in the practice of the revolutionary class struggle and revolutionary national struggle, as well as in the practice of scientific experiment. This is the process of testing and developing theory, the continuation of the whole process of knowledge."[1]

Hence the task of raising knowledge to the level of knowledge of the essence of things is the task of bringing about a revolution in human practice, in man's power to master nature and change

[1] Mao Tse-tung, *loc. cit.*

it, to direct his own life and change it. The task of knowledge is "to start from perceptual knowledge and actively develop it into rational knowledge, and then, starting from rational knowledge, actively direct revolutionary practice so as to remould the subjective and objective world."[1]

Things in Themselves

It follows from this analysis of the growth of knowledge that, in all its stages, it is the growth of the faithful reflection in human consciousness of the real, objective world.

Many philosophers have maintained that our knowledge is limited to the appearances of things in our own minds, and that "things in themselves", things as they really are "in themselves" and independently of how they appear to us, the essential nature of things, must be unknowable. According to such philosophers there is an impassable gulf between the data of sense given in our consciousness on the one hand and the things existing independently of our consciousness, things in themselves, on the other hand. And many not only deny that we can know things in themselves but also that such things exist at all.

And yet already in judgments directly based on perception we are gaining knowledge of things in themselves—not in the first place complete or profound knowledge but knowledge at least of various separate aspects and external relations of things. We gain this knowledge precisely by means of the data of sense. And when by further investigation and reasoning we reach conclusions about the essential properties and relations and laws of motion of things, then we are gaining deeper knowledge of the very same things in themselves which before we knew only superficially.

There is, then, no gulf between things in themselves and their appearances or "phenomena". We know things in themselves precisely by means of their appearances to us, and the more we study the appearances the more we can find out about the things in themselves. Nor is there any gulf between

[1] *Ibid.*

the appearances of things and their essence, since the appearance is a manifestation of the essence, and we do not know the essence separately from the appearance but only through it. " If you know all the qualities of a thing, you know the thing itself ", wrote Engels.[1] We know things in themselves by practice and study. By finding out what we can do with things, and by studying the various appearances of their various aspects under many conditions, we gain more and more knowledge of the things themselves.

Hence all our knowledge is knowledge of things in themselves, which certainly exist and are certainly knowable. " The materialist affirms the existence and knowability of things in themselves."[2] First we know things in themselves superficially through perception, and then more deeply and comprehensively by thought operating with the data of perception. There is, and can be, no difference between the things known to us and things in themselves. The only difference is between what is known and what is not yet known, and between what is known only superficially in certain of its aspects and what is known more thoroughly.

Knowledge is Both Limited and Limitless

Are there, then, limits to human knowledge, or has it no limits ?

At any particular stage in the development of humanity knowledge comes up against limits set by the necessarily limited character of the experience available and of the existing means of obtaining knowledge.

But humanity advances precisely by overcoming such limits. New experience throws down the limits of old experience ; new techniques, new means of obtaining knowledge throw down the limits of old techniques and old means of obtaining knowledge.

New limits then once again appear. But there is no more reason to suppose these new limits absolute and final than

[1] Engels, *Socialism, Utopian and Scientific*, Introduction.
[2] Lenin, *loc. cit.*, ch. 2, section 2.

there was to suppose the old ones absolute and final. At every stage there are people who think that the limit has been reached and who look no further. But there are always, sooner or later, other people who throw down those limits and boldly advance beyond them to new limits.

Therefore knowledge is always limited, and is at the same time limitless.

In other words, the known is always bounded by the unknown, but not by the unknowable.

For example, it was impossible for people in feudal society to know anything about socialist society and its laws, to formulate the truth about socialism and the transition from socialism to communism. This became possible only with the development of capitalist society; only then did the means become available for forming a scientific conception of socialism. Similarly it is impossible for us today to know how a fully communist society, after it is established, will further develop; but in due course people will be able to ascertain the truth about this further development and its laws.

Again, it was impossible to gain knowledge of the atom and its structure before the invention of modern techniques of electronics. Today with these techniques we have passed what were once thought to be the limits of all possible physical knowledge. These techniques themselves involve, however, their own limits to physical knowledge—so that now some physicists assert the impossibility of ever knowing anything about, for example, the structure of the electron. But it would be both dogmatic and short-sighted to assert that these limits are any more absolute than were the once insurmountable limits of other techniques in the past. "While yesterday the profundity of this knowledge did not go beyond the atom, and today does not go beyond the electron," wrote Lenin, ". . . dialectical materialism insists on the temporary, relative, approximate character of all these *milestones* in the knowledge of nature gained by the progressing science of man. The electron is as *inexhaustible* as the atom, nature is infinite. . . ."[1]

[1] Lenin, *loc. cit.*, ch. 5, section 2.

At every stage and in all circumstances knowledge is incomplete and provisional, conditioned and limited by the historical circumstances under which it was acquired, including the means and methods used for gaining it and the historically conditioned assumptions and categories used in the formulation of ideas and conclusions.

But this development of knowledge, every stage of which has such a conditioned character, is a development of knowledge of the real material world, the discovery of interconnections and laws of motion of real material processes, including human society and human consciousness. It is a progressive development, in which the bounds of knowledge are stage by stage enlarged, in which the agreement of ideas and theories with objective reality is stage by stage increased, and in which stage by stage what was provisional and hypothetical gives place to what is assured and verified.

The progress of knowledge always comes up against barriers which arise from the limitations of existing knowledge and existing practice. But there are no impassable barriers. While the progress of knowledge always faces barriers to further advance, knowledge progresses precisely by finding how to get over them. There are no limits to knowledge, no unknowable things, no mystery or secret of the universe, nothing which cannot in principle be known and explained.

CHAPTER THIRTEEN

NECESSITY AND FREEDOM

Rational knowledge reveals the necessity of things, and at the same time that the necessary is always realised through the accidental. By the acquisition of knowledge we gain freedom which consists in the control over ourselves and over external nature founded on knowledge of necessity. We are free when on the basis of knowledge we decide what to do and exert conscious control over the factors influencing the fulfilment of our aim.

Necessity and Accident

WHEN knowledge advances to the stage of rational knowledge which grasps the essence and inner connections of things, then we begin to understand the aspect of *necessity* which belongs to phenomena of both nature and society.

We call that necessary which from the nature of the case could not be otherwise. When the essential nature of a thing is such that it is bound to manifest certain characteristics and not others, and to develop in a certain way and not in another, then those characteristics and that development are understood as necessary.

The conception of the necessary is linked with that of the essential. In general, in so far as we gain knowledge of the essential characteristics, inner connections and laws of development of things, we are able to state not merely what the facts are but to explain them, to understand the reasons for them, to comprehend their necessity.

In the field of natural science, for example, the discoveries of Newton concerning the principles of mechanics revealed the necessity of many phenomena of nature. Thus among other things Newton's principles demonstrated the necessity of certain features of the solar system of which the earth is a part. It is a fact, for instance, that the planets move round the sun in elliptical orbits. This fact was established by Kepler. But the necessity of Kepler's law of planetary motion was demonstrated by Newton, whose analysis of the mechanics of the solar system showed that from the very nature of the forces operating in such a system the planets were bound to move in elliptical orbits, and not in circles or any other kind of orbit. Thus the general character of the solar system is not accidental— it is a necessary consequence of the essential nature of such a system, of its inner connection and laws of development.

Again, to take an example from social life, it is a fact that in Britain the police always intervene in industrial disputes on the side of the employers. From the point of view of superficial observation, this is merely a fact. But yet it is not accidental. For once we have grasped the essential nature of the contemporary British State as a capitalist state, then we can understand that if the police help the employers this is no accident but a necessary consequence of the capitalist regime.

If, however, we come to understand the necessity of certain aspects of things, and of certain types of events, this does not mean that everything is understood as necessary, that there is no place left in the world for *accident*. On the contrary, particular events always have a chance or accidental character. The recognition of necessity in things is inseparable from the recognition at the same time of accident.

For example, the police in a capitalist state necessarily serve the capitalist class. But they do not necessarily wear blue uniforms. On the contrary, they could serve the capitalists just as well in uniforms of some other colour ; and so the fact that the British police wear blue uniforms is an accident—it is due to accidental, inessential circumstances.

Similarly, while it is a necessary feature of the solar system that the earth moves round the sun in an elliptical orbit, it is not a necessary feature that the earth is the exact size it is : its exact size is due to accidental, inessential circumstances.

From the point of view of superficial observation, everything appears accidental. We are simply confronted with observed facts and external connections between them. As we have not yet grasped the laws of change and interconnection which govern and manifest themselves in the things we are observing, every fact we observe is apprehended simply as a fact which could quite well have been otherwise. " Every fact could be the case or not be the case, and everything else remain the same " :[1] such is the conclusion of a superficial way of viewing things.

But profounder investigation reveals that " where on the surface accident holds sway, there actually it is always governed by inner, hidden laws and it is only a matter of discovering these laws."[2]

Their discovery does not, however, eliminate the conception of the accidental. Rather does it reveal that the necessary features of things manifest themselves through a series of accidents, and that the accidental, on the other hand, is always governed by the necessary.

Thus it is a historical necessity that in the development of society capitalism should be superseded by socialism. Exactly when and how this revolution takes place involves a series of accidental circumstances, but the development of these circumstances is, in turn, governed by historical necessity.

Similarly in nature, the development of matter necessarily follows a certain path, though exactly when and how in a particular material system the different stages of development are realised, or whether in particular cases they are realised at all, depends upon accidental, inessential circumstances.

So, dealing with the inter-relation of accident and necessity in nature, Engels wrote that the solar system " was produced in a natural way by transformations of motion which are by nature inherent in moving matter, and the conditions of which therefore also must be reproduced by matter, even if only after millions and millions of years and more or less by

---

[1] L. Wittgenstein, *Tractatus Logico-Philosophicus*, 1.21.
[2] Engels, *Ludwig Feuerbach*, ch. 4.

chance but with the necessity that is also inherent in chance."[1] And he understood the emergence of consciousness, as the highest form of motion of matter, in the same way. " It is the nature of matter to advance to the evolution of thinking beings ; hence, too, this always necessarily occurs wherever the conditions for it (not necessarily identical at all places and times) are present."[2]

Engels therefore concluded that " what is maintained to be necessary is composed of sheer accidents, and the so-called accidental is the form behind which necessity hides itself".[3]

If the necessary is that which from the nature of the case could not be otherwise, the accidental is that which could be otherwise. Both aspects are always present in everything. In general, it is certain overall characteristics of events, and the overall character of their outcome, which are necessary. On the other hand, the details, the particular features of individual events, and the consequent detailed, particular features of their outcome, are not necessary but accidental. It is in this sense that " what is necessary is composed of accidents ". It is precisely in the accidental details that the inherently necessary manifests itself, and, accidental in themselves, they are at the same time shaped and governed by what is necessary.

Necessity, Accident and Causality

The discovery of necessity in nature and society is bound up with the discovery of causes and of the laws governing the relationship of causes and effects. What is necessary is necessary because of the operation of causes. If there were things which came into being without any causes, if there were events which took place absolutely at random and without regulation by causal laws, then there could be no necessity discoverable in such things and events.

So if a certain characteristic is a necessary characteristic of certain events, and if a certain result is their necessary outcome,

---

[1] Engels, *Dialectics of Nature*, Introduction.
[2] Engels, *loc. cit.*, Notes.
[3] Engels, *Ludwig Feuerbach*, ch. 4.

this is consequent upon the nature of the causal processes which operate in these events. To get to understand the necessity inherent in events is to reach a profound knowledge of the causal processes operating in them.

For example, if capitalism will necessarily be superseded by socialism, this is because the causes of the transition from capitalism to socialism are generated within the capitalist system, and nothing can stop them from operating. If we profoundly know the nature of capitalism, then we know that such causes are present and cannot but be present and continue to operate in such a system.

At the same time, the knowledge of causes also enables us to understand the accidental features of things.

The causes of socialism, for example, come into being and operate within capitalism, and so the outcome of socialism is known to be necessary. But the particular features of these causes are accidental. There is no necessity about them. Thus it is necessary that the working class should increase in numbers and organisation as capitalism develops ; this is bound to happen, and is one of the causes why capitalism will give rise to socialism. But while the continued development of capitalism necessarily implies that there will be more workers and that they will organise and eventually overthrow the system, it does not necessarily imply that, say, Mr. Jones and Mr. Smith will join an organisation and play a prominent part as leaders of the movement. There are bound to be leaders, but whether a particular child of particular parents will become a leader depends on many accidental factors. Such accidental factors, however, are, in the aggregate and in the long run, bound to have the result that leaders will arise.

Thus the operation of causality brings it about that there is both necessity and accident in the world, and that the necessary manifests itself through the accidental.

It follows that it is wrong to assert, as has often been asserted, that when a cause has been assigned for anything, then that thing has thereby been shown to be necessary. It is equally wrong to define the accidental as that which happens without a cause. All events have causes, necessary events and accidents alike. Merely to trace something back to its remote causes is not to prove its necessity, for accident is at work right throughout the chain of events. If something is necessary, this is not a consequence of particular causes but of general laws.

The inter-relation of accident and necessity in events is grasped, then, as a consequence of the advance of knowledge from the external to the internal connections of things, from appearance to essence, from superficial observation and correlation of facts to investigation of the real dialectic of development. Then we see that necessary consequences of the essential nature of things manifest themselves through a series of accidental circumstances, and that accidental events are conditioned and governed by an internal necessity and contribute to bringing about a necessary outcome.

Necessity and Freedom in Human Practice

We have considered the inter-relation of necessity and accident and how both arise from the universal operation of causality in nature and society. Now we shall consider the bearing of these conclusions on practical life.

When we carry out practical activities, do we possess any freedom in what we are doing or is it all necessarily determined independently of our will? This is the question we must now answer. And as it is sometimes thought that necessity and accident are incompatible opposites, such that where the one is present the other must be absent, so the same thing is often thought about necessity and freedom. It is thought that where necessity is present there can be no freedom and that, on the other hand, if we do act freely then we must somehow have escaped from necessity.

If this idea were correct, then human freedom would be an illusion. All men's activities, like everything else in the world, are in all respects governed by causal laws. The operations of causality give rise to necessary characteristics of events and determine their necessary outcome; and this applies as much to human actions as to anything else, so that men can never make themselves independent of necessity in nature and society. But it is wrong to oppose freedom and necessity as incompatibles. On the contrary, necessity gives rise to freedom and is its precondition.

The operation of natural and social laws and the necessities consequent on this are independent of our will and of our consciousness. Hence whatever we may think or desire or decide, our actions are always determined in accordance with the laws of nature in general and of our own nature in particular, and conform, in their carrying out and in their consequences, to the dictates of necessity.

Man is himself a part of nature, and " the necessity of nature is primary, and human will and mind secondary. The latter must necessarily and inevitably adapt themselves to the former."[1]

What characterises human practice, however, and distinguishes it from animal behaviour, is that men in the course of their social practice gain knowledge of necessity, in the first place of necessity in nature, and so learn to act on that knowledge and to use it to produce intended aims, to realise their own purposes.

This begins with the production process itself, in which man " sets in motion the natural forces of his body in order to appropriate nature's productions in a form adapted to his own wants ", and so " realises a purpose of his own."[2]

Consequently men are not, like the animals, constrained to follow a predetermined pattern of behaviour. They do not, like the animals, simply adapt themselves to their environment, but also by their own volition adapt their environment to themselves. They *make themselves free* to seek and realise ends which they themselves have conceived and willed. And in so doing they also change themselves, change their own nature.

But the mastery over nature, which distinguishes man from the animals, does not imply the least independence of man from natural law and natural necessity. On the contrary, what it depends on is not the abrogation of natural laws and natural necessity but knowledge and conscious utilisation of them.

[1] Lenin, *Materialism and Empirio-Criticism*, ch. 3, section 6.
[2] Marx, *Capital*, Vol. I, ch. 7, section 1.

Similarly, when men learn also to control and plan their own social life in order to satisfy their material and cultural requirements, this again does not imply that they have achieved independence of the objective laws of society, of social necessity. On the contrary, what it depends on is not the abrogation of objective social laws but knowledge and conscious utilisation of these laws—not the ending of necessity in society but its recognition, and the direction of social activity in accordance with that recognition of necessity.

" Marxism regards laws of science—whether they be laws of natural science or laws of political economy—as the reflection of objective processes which take place independently of the will of man ", wrote Stalin. " Man may discover these laws, get to know them, study them, reckon with them in his activities and utilise them in the interests of society, but he cannot change or abolish them."[1]

Men are therefore never, in any respect, in any of their activities, independent of natural or social laws and of their necessary consequences. It follows that in so far as they lack knowledge of these laws and of their consequences, they are constrained and unfree. These laws with their necessary consequences then assert themselves as an alien power, with unexpected or destructive effects, frustrating human purposes. But in so far as men gain knowledge of these laws and knowledge of their necessary consequences, they can learn to utilise them for their own purposes. They can " learn to apply them with full understanding, utilise them in the interests of society, and thus subjugate them, secure mastery over them."[2]

Freedom does not consist in cutting loose from the operations of causality but in understanding them. It does not depend on getting rid of necessity but on getting knowledge of it.

There is, therefore, no incompatibility between the existence of necessity and of human freedom. On the contrary, as we have stated, necessity gives rise to freedom, namely, when men gain knowledge of necessity and so can recognise it and

[1] Stalin, *Economic Problems of Socialism in the U.S.S.R.*
[2] *Ibid.*

make their decisions in the light of real understanding of what they are doing.

What is more, as we have also stated, so far from being in opposition to human freedom, the existence of necessity is its precondition.

What would happen if there were no causal laws in nature and society, if there were no objective necessity regulating the course of events? In that case, anything could happen. We could not decide upon or carry out even the simplest actions, for we could never know what to do in order to secure the results we intended. We would not possess even the freedom to make a cup of tea, for example, for we would never know whether the water would boil or, when we poured it into the teapot, what the resulting brew would turn out like. Still less could we carry out any more complex social activities, for everything would be in chaos. In fact, we could not exist at all.

It is only because things *are* subject to laws, because objective necessity *does* exist in nature and society, that we are able to decide upon definite actions and to carry them out. This is the condition for human freedom. And that freedom is realised in proportion as we extend our knowledge and, consequently, our ability to make decisions on the basis of knowledge and so to carry them into effect.

Further, when we do know the laws governing things, then we can carry out activities in relation to them which we could not carry out without such knowledge. For example, people often dreamed about flying, but until recently considered that the laws of nature prevented them from being able to fly. When, however, we discovered the laws governing flying, then we were able to construct the means of flight. In many such cases, knowledge of the laws which have given rise to certain limitations on our action enables us in practice to transcend those limitations.

Knowledge as the Means to Human Freedom

But are not our own actions determined by various causes and are they not therefore subject to an overriding necessity? How, then, can we be free?

It is true that we ourselves are the products of definite conditions, would have been different had those conditions been different, and act according to the necessity of our own circumstances and our own nature. But this does not in the least contradict the possibility of our being free agents.

Whatever we do, there was some cause of our doing it. If this cause was an external force of some kind, acting on us in such a way as to make us do something without the intervention of any act of will on our part, then certainly in such a case we are constrained and not free. For example, if someone in a crowd pushes me in such a way that I push someone else, then in this case I am not a free agent. The question of freedom only comes in when we do things of our own volition—that is to say, when the cause of what we do is our own act of will. But how is our own will determined? If it is determined by various external forces operating on and moulding our will so as to effect purposes which are not our own, then we still lack freedom. In that case we may have the illusion of acting freely, but it is only an illusion. But lastly, if our will is determined by our knowledge of the circumstances of our action and of what must be done to realise a purpose which we have made our own, then in that case we not only feel free but really are free.

Such a quality of free operation is not inherent in the will but comes into being. And its coming into being and the extent of its development follow in turn from definite causes which come into operation in social life.

As a result of the operation of the laws of our own development, as a result of the necessities of our own nature, we gain knowledge of external things and of our own nature and requirements, and then we act on the basis of such knowledge. In proportion as this takes place, what we do follows from our own conscious decisions based on knowledge of our own requirements and of how to realise them. And so we are free. What other sort of freedom do we expect or can we desire?

This, incidentally, is a point which was, in its essentials, made clear long ago by the great materialist philosopher Spinoza, when he pointed out that human actions, like all other things, are determined by prior causes ; and that men are free not when their actions take place without causes but when their actions are determined by their knowledge of their own requirements and of how to realise them.[1]

" Freedom does not consist in the dream of independence of natural laws ", wrote Engels, " but in the knowledge of these laws, and in the possibility this gives of systematically making them work towards definite ends. This holds good in relation both to the laws of external nature and to those which govern the bodily and mental life of men themselves—two classes of laws which we can separate from each other at most only in thought and not in reality. Freedom of the will therefore means nothing but the capacity to make decisions with real knowledge of the subject. . . . Freedom therefore consists or the control over ourselves and over external nature which is founded on the knowledge of natural necessity."[2]

Human knowledge, then, is an essential means to human freedom. If knowledge depends on practice, the growth of knowledge has also a transforming effect on practice. Practice based on knowledge is another thing from practice not based on knowledge. For in so far as we know the properties and laws of things, we can in practice master them—make them subject to us, instead of we being subject to them. The growth of knowledge, a product of man's striving to master nature and to organise his own social life, contributes step by step to the realisation of that mastery and to the building of higher forms of social organisation, to the realisation of the possibility of a full and free life for all.

Freedom and Accident

We have already considered the linkage in nature and society of necessity and accident, and have seen that necessity realises itself through a series of accidents. To act freely on the basis of knowledge further means, then, that we, as conscious agents,

[1] See B. de Spinoza, *Ethics*.
[2] Engels, *Anti-Duhring*, Part I, ch. 11.

must exercise practical control over these accidents, so as to eliminate the accidental or chance element in the determination of the results of our activity and make those results fully conform with our own intentions. In other words, the exercise of our freedom of action means that, in carrying out activities directed to a definite end, we, on the basis of our knowledge of the laws of the subject of our action, exercise such control over the subject that the operations of chance are eliminated in the determination of the result.

Thus while the realisation of freedom of human action does not in any sense mean getting rid of necessity, it does, in a certain sense, mean getting rid of accident, or eliminating chance.

In carrying out an undertaking we should, as everyone knows, not leave to chance anything which affects the success of the undertaking. If we do, then the success of the undertaking is jeopardised. If it succeeds, that is due to luck and not to judgment; circumstances have brought about success for us, and it was not we who by our own deliberate actions achieved success for ourselves. But circumstances cannot generally be relied on to be so favourable.

Those organising street-corner meetings, for example, sometimes forget to arrange for anyone to bring the platform along. They leave it to chance, and so occasionally find themselves without a platform. Sometimes they may even be without a speaker for the same reason. Naturally enough, anyone who organises anything has the job of taking all the factors affecting the success of the undertaking into account and leaving none of them to chance.

The elementary characteristics of free action, namely, knowledge of necessity and elimination of chance, are exemplified in the labour process, the fundamental process of human activity.

In the labour process man by his work, using the instruments of labour, operates on the subject of the work to effect a designed alteration in it. To do this he has to know and reckon with the necessary characteristics of the subject of work, and he has also to eliminate the effects of chance on the subject of work.

The more large-scale and ambitious grow the undertakings

of human labour, the more does man succeed in eliminating the factor of chance in his undertakings.

This is a very important consideration in any engineering work. To build a bridge, for instance, the engineers base their plans on their knowledge of the essential nature of the location and of the materials employed, and on a reckoning with the various chance factors to which the structure may be subjected. An example of failure to reckon with chance was recently afforded by the sea defences on the east coast of England. Those who were responsible for these defences had omitted to reckon with the chance that an exceptionally high tide might coincide with an exceptionally strong east wind. When this chance coincidence took place, the sea burst through the defences. But if sea defences, or any other engineering works, are properly planned, then such chances are reckoned with and their effects eliminated.

One of the most chancy factors affecting men's undertakings is the weather. And so agricultural undertakings are constantly at the mercy of the weather. One of the principal features of the large-scale food production plans in the socialist Soviet Union is, partly to control the weather, and partly to counteract its adverse effects in so far as it remains outside direct control. Shelter belts fulfil just these objects. They serve partly to control the weather and partly to protect crops from bad weather. By such means Soviet people freely go ahead regularly to produce high crop yields.

The Elements of Conscious Control

By considering such examples we can draw some further conclusions about the inter-relation of necessity, accident and human freedom.

To say that freedom entails the elimination of chances does not mean, of course, that by the exercise of freedom we somehow contrive to do away with the linkage of accident and necessity. The operation of accident or chance, and its linkage with necessity, is an objective fact, a universal feature of events in both nature and society, which we have to reckon with and to which we have to adapt our actions. It exists independently of ourselves and we can by no means do away with or alter it. What we have to do to realise freedom of action is, through knowledge of necessity, to bring a whole process, including the chances inherent in it, under our control and so direct it to an end decided by ourselves. So eliminating chance means controlling it, so as to direct its operation and to render the outcome no longer accidental. This is done by means of (a) exercising a direct control over chance factors and (b) exercising foresight and taking precautions to cope with them in so far as they remain outside direct control. This is why a socialist economic plan, for example, must always include the building up of " reserves ".

One aspect of foresight in relation to chance is expressed in the saying, " Heads I win, tails you lose". If such a situation can be brought into being, then I have ensured that I win. If the outcome depends on the accident of the spin of a coin, then it is decided independently of man's volition and not by man's volition. But if it is arranged that whatever chances, some suitable precaution has been contrived to bring about the desired outcome, then it is man's volition that decides the outcome. If people are making bets, this is called cheating ; but we do not consider it cheating in relation to nature. Thus, for example, the success of a crop planted in the open steppes may depend on the chance of whether or not a dry wind blows ; if it blows, the crop suffers. To plant a shelter belt is to eliminate this contingency. Then if the wind blows the crop is protected, and if it does not blow the crop is all right anyway. It is a case of " Heads I win, tails you lose "—chance is defeated.

Another aspect of eliminating chance is illustrated by spinning a coin in which we have been careful to introduce a bias. And the use of shelter belts exemplifies this aspect too. They conserve moisture and make the climate wetter, and in this way introduce a bias into the weather.

We have seen that necessity realises itself through a series of accidents, and also that accidental events are governed by an internal necessity. When this point is grasped in a practical way, and when we are equipped with knowledge of the laws of the subject of our activities, then we are in a position to reckon with and control the accidental factors inherent in the subject, so that we ourselves direct them to a necessary outcome in accordance with our intentions.

This further requires that our knowledge should be not only knowledge of the inevitable but also of the probable. In relation to a given process, for instance, we must not only know what effect universally follows from what cause, so that by bringing the cause into being we can ensure the corresponding effect; but we must also know the probabilities of various causes coming into operation and of various effects following. This enables us to judge how to act in order to control the whole process, including its accidental features.

Judgments of probability express our expectation of the occurrence of accidents. According to some theories, probability is purely subjective, in the sense that a judgment of probability is an expression of nothing but our own subjective uncertainty or lack of knowledge. But on the contrary, the idea of probability reflects an objective reality—or rather, one aspect of objective reality—namely, the operation of accidental causes in a whole sequence of events or in an aggregate of instances. This is just as much an objective reality as the operation of a single cause on a single occasion, which is not a subject of probability.

In proportion as we know the probabilities inherent in events and can arrive at correct judgments of probability, we are able the better to reckon with *all* the factors operating in the course of a whole process, including the accidental factors, and so to direct the whole process towards a definite end.

To sum up.

Freedom is control over ourselves and over external nature which is founded on knowledge of necessity. Such knowledge also requires that we know what chance factors enter into the process with which we are concerned, and the probabilities characterising their operation, so that we can (*a*) control the operation of chance and (*b*) take precautions to meet its operation in so far as we do not control it, as a result of which the whole process is directed to a desired end.

" Chance is only the one pole of a relation whose other pole is called ' necessity '," wrote Engels. ". . . The more a social activity, a series of social processes, becomes too powerful for men's conscious control and grows above their heads, and the more it appears a matter of pure chance, then all the more surely within this chance the laws peculiar to it and inherent in it assert themselves as if by natural necessity."[1]

When events in which we are concerned thus take place without our conscious control over them, then the outcome is determined by a natural necessity realised through a series of accidents. But in proportion as we do achieve a conscious control over events, it is we ourselves who consciously determine their course, by acting on our knowledge of the laws of such events and of the factors influencing the outcome.

[1] Engels, *The Origin of the Family, etc.*, ch. 9.

CHAPTER FOURTEEN

THE REALISATION OF FREEDOM

People are not born free but gradually win freedom. Freedom is won and advanced through struggle for mastery over nature and through class struggle. In class society, the freedom actually won and possessed by different classes, and the restrictions on their freedom, differ in concrete ways, corresponding to the position and aims of the classes. The struggle for freedom is in essence people's struggle to be able to satisfy their own requirements; starting from merely animal conditions of existence, mankind continually advances on the road of the realisation of freedom, which leads to communist society. The stages of the evolution of freedom are also stages in the evolution of morality.

The Winning of Freedom

MOST of the theoretical difficulties people run into when thinking of the problem of freedom result from thinking that freedom is an innate quality of the will. But freedom is not an innate quality of the will, nor is it any sort of gift or endowment which God or nature has bestowed upon man. It is something which is *won*—and which is won gradually, bit by bit, created and realised in the course of ages of human social activity.

J. J. Rousseau began his book on *The Social Contract* with the famous words, " Man is born free ". But man is not born free. On the contrary, man is born with no freedom whatever, but is born as a creature determined by circumstances independent of his will. But thanks to his social life and the laws of its development, he gradually develops in social practice those capacities which make him *become* free. This he does in struggle with external nature, in social and class struggle, and also in individual struggle. He creates for himself and wins for himself such freedom as he possesses, and so he can never possess more than he has created and won for himself.

Freedom is not an innate quality, nor is it an " all or none " affair. Metaphysicians argue that either we are free or else we are not free. This is to forget that we may be free in some respects but not in others, and that we may be more or less free.

In the argument between voluntarism, which says that the will is not determined, and determinism, which says that the will *is* determined, Marxism takes the determinist side, since every act of will has a cause. But the important question is not that of whether our actions are determined—since there is no doubt that they are determined—but of how and by what they are determined—by external causes or by our own knowledge of our needs and of how to satisfy them. When the question is put like this, then it is evident that freedom is a matter of degree. We make ourselves free only in so far as we bring it about that our own conscious decision based on knowledge is the thing which determines what we do and achieve. But such freedom can seldom if ever be absolute. The *more* it is our own decision based on knowledge which determines our actions and their outcome, and the *less* they are decided for us by other factors, the *greater* is the *degree of freedom of action* which we have achieved.

Freedom of the Individual and Freedom in Society

Freedom is something which is realised by the individual. It is not mankind in general, or society, that is free, but individuals who are free.

But in the first place, the individual realises freedom only through society. The means to freedom is knowledge, and this is social. The freedom of the individual depends on the acquirements of the society to which he belongs, on the education and assistance which society has afforded him, and also on the extent to which, in society, he can co-operate with others and get them to co-operate with him.

In the second place, therefore, the individual attains to that degree of freedom which has been attained by and is permitted to him by the society to which he belongs. The scope of his freedom is dependent on the acquirements of his society, but it is also dependent on how far society will permit him to share in and make use of those acquirements. The potential scope of his freedom is as great as the existing social knowledge and the means discovered to utilise it. At the same time, his actual enjoyment of this potential freedom may be denied to him by limitations placed by society on his own acquirements and his own actions.

The freedom of individuals, then, depends upon the positive acquirements of society and the opportunities society affords to individuals to utilise those acquirements. This being so, individuals struggle together—both with one another and against one another—for a higher degree of freedom. And they thereby raise the degree of freedom possessed by all individuals and realised by them in society.

It follows, then, that an individual develops as a free agent in the course of his life, corresponding to the education, incentives and opportunities afforded him by society. And similarly, men in society have developed human freedom in the course of social evolution. Mankind gradually advances on the road of greater freedom of action. This freedom of action is, indeed, a measure or criterion of social progress.

The Struggle for Freedom

In primitive societies, people's freedom is restricted mainly by their lack of mastery over nature. They are very much at the mercy of external nature, and the savage's existence is to a very great extent determined for him by external conditions, as is the case with animals.

As civilisation has developed, so has people's mastery over nature developed. Hence their freedom in this respect has become less and less restricted, more and more enlarged. But a new restriction has come into operation. In civilised societies hitherto, people's freedom has been restricted by social circumstances, and in particular by the oppression of one class by another. Hence as the freedom associated with the mastery over nature has increased, so has it been offset by class oppression. This means that people have been exploited and coerced, and at the same time have been denied the opportunity of utilising for their own interests the knowledge and power which exist in society.

The English youth today, for example, are sent to fight in colonial wars. This is something which not only serves to maintain a restriction on the freedom of the people in the colonies but also restricts the freedom of the British youth to live and enjoy their own lives. If the knowledge and resources which are put into preparing and waging such wars were used by the colonial people and by the majority of the British people for our own welfare, then we could do and enjoy many things which we cannot do and cannot enjoy at present. This also is a restriction on our freedom.

If people are to be free, then neither in their economic activities nor in any other of their activities should they be constrained to work or to act or to think contrary to their own interests, to the detriment of their own essential requirements, by external pressure and for the benefit of others. And they should not be denied the opportunity of utilising all society offers for the satisfaction of their requirements. Such conditions are a negation of people's freedom. Their prevalence hitherto has been due to the division of society into exploiting and exploited classes.

Metaphysical philosophers have carefully separated the question of the so-called freedom of the will from the question of economic and political freedom, and this separation has helped them to mislead people about both. But in fact these are not separate questions but two aspects of the one question of men's struggle for freedom. In a society in which one class exploits another, the main part of the struggle for freedom is the struggle to throw off the existing forms of exploitation and oppression. And it is in this struggle that men act freely, make themselves free and enlarge the frontiers of human freedom. A passive slave is simply a slave, but a slave in revolt is acting as a free man even though he still wears his chains. Such people are pioneers of human freedom.

It follows that, in class society, freedom and the winning of freedom has always a class background to it. And the concept of freedom has therefore a class significance. In the first place, the freedom which has been won and realised at any stage, and also the lack of freedom, is always the freedom or lack of freedom of definite classes. In the second place, the freedom or lack of freedom of one class differs in concrete ways from the freedom or lack of freedom of another class; and consequently different classes also have different ideas of what constitutes freedom.

Human freedom has been constantly advanced by the class struggle, and various classes, striving to realise their own aims and to make themselves free to pursue those aims, have advanced the freedom of people generally from one stage to another. Each stage is realised as a result of struggle against the restrictions on freedom placed by a definite system of class rule, and in turn produces its own restrictions on freedom.

Thus, for example, feudal rule and serfdom were ended as a result of the struggle led by the bourgeoisie against feudal restrictions. This was a step forward in men's freedom. It brought with it new forms of exploitation and oppression, but it also brought new advances, the winning of broader political rights and liberties, new and more powerful organisation, advances in knowledge and culture. At the same time, it has meant in practice different things for the two main classes of capitalist society. The capitalist class is concerned to maintain its rule and increase its profits. The working class, on the other hand, is confronted with the task of getting rid of capitalist rule and capitalist exploitation, and of using the freedom which it has already won in order to advance to a higher order of freedom.

Similarly, restrictions of freedom are experienced differently by the different classes. Every system of exploitation imposes definite forms of coercion and oppression on the exploited; and the working class today, for example, experiences this. At the same time, each ruling class, which seems to itself to have realised its own freedom by exploiting others, finds in practice that its freedom is largely illusory. The bourgeoisie, for example, find themselves enslaved by the laws of their own system, and must go on accumulating capital, competing with one another and fighting with one another to the end.

To a poor family today, debating whether to exercise their free will in paying the rent or buying some food, it often seems that a rich capitalist is far freer than they are. They do not realise the extent to which the unfortunate man is the slave of his own business, suffering high blood pressure and perpetual worry and frustration. If they did, simple humanity might prompt them to set him free from these cares, and do themselves a bit of good too, by taking over his business from him and allowing him the freedom of honest work. Members of various exploiting classes have often believed that riches and power would give them complete freedom. But even their own philosophers have sadly but truly pointed out to them that riches and power enslave their possessors at the same time as they are engaged in enslaving others.

From Lack of Freedom to Freedom

The struggle for freedom means in essence people's struggle to be able to satisfy their own requirements, material and cultural, for which is needed knowledge of those requirements and of how to satisfy them, and the power to effect that satisfaction.

When in socialist society people, having already greatly expanded their mastery over nature, bring their own social organisation under their own conscious control by virtue of the social ownership of the means of production, then a decisive step forward is realised in human freedom. In socialist society, when there is no exploitation of man by man and when the means of production are common property and are utilised for the purpose of satisfying the requirements of every individual, people begin less to struggle for freedom than to enjoy it and learn how to go forward to exercise it to the full. And when in communist society people finally do away with all traces of the subordination of people to their own means of production and products, then people will have attained to the highest degree of freedom we can envisage. Then, as Engels put it, " for the first time man, in a certain sense, is finally marked off from the rest of the animal kingdom, and emerges from mere animal conditions of existence into really human ones. . . . It is the ascent of man from the kingdom of necessity to the kingdom of freedom."[1]

We can say that people started off from mere animal conditions of existence, but began to create conditions of freedom when they first began social production—that is to say, when they began to use tools and implements to change things, in accordance with the objective laws of nature, with conscious intent to satisfy their own requirements.

In producing, people have entered into relations of production, and in the course of ages of struggle to satisfy their own ever growing requirements they have continually advanced their knowledge and consequently their control over their own affairs and over external nature. This struggle has advanced through a series of stages, in each of which people have changed their relations of production to correspond with the development of their forces of production, and in each of which different classes have enlarged their own sphere of free activity only at the cost of new forms of domination of one class over another and of new forms of subjection to the objective laws of their own social organisation. At length the class struggle has reached that stage in which the struggle of the exploited class for its own emancipation will finally emancipate society at large from all exploitation and oppression, and so will bring about conditions in which men's own social organisation comes under their own conscious, social control and becomes the result of their own free action. Then, too, the labour process, by which men began their journey to freedom but which became a process of enslavement, will become the conscious means by which they achieve the satisfaction of all their needs ; and by

[1] Engels, *Socialism, Utopian and Scientific*, ch. 3.

limiting the hours of labour each will be able freely to develop and enjoy the exercise of all his capacities.

In this way, by a process which is entirely law governed, which is determined at every point by the operation of objective laws, people gradually emerge from a condition of complete lack of freedom, when what they do and achieve is not determined by their own conscious decision but by their circumstances, and gradually win freedom, attaining at length a condition in which individually and collectively they can consciously decide their own fate on the basis of knowledge of their own needs and of conscious control over the conditions for their satisfaction.

Morality

The stages of the evolution of freedom are closely connected with the evolution of morality, or ethics. The development of morals is, in fact, one side or aspect of the development of freedom, and the various stages of the development of moral ideas are so many stages of the evolution of human freedom.

Many moral philosophers have observed that morality is an expression of freedom and that the moral life has meaning only in so far as people are acting freely. And of course, if all our actions were merely the determined consequences of external causes, then there would be no sense in calling them right or wrong, or in saying that we had a duty to do one thing rather than another, since in that case we could not help what we did. In this, these philosophers were evidently right. What they did not observe is that freedom is something which develops socially on the basis of the activities of definite classes, and that the same is true of morals.

Human morality is not an expression of some eternal moral law decreed by heaven and somehow revealed to mankind; nor is it, as Kant imagined, the expression of a " categorical imperative " inherent in the human will; but it is a natural product of men's social organisation. Since men live in society, they necessarily evolve a moral code to regulate their mutual relations and activities in society. This assumes in relation to individuals the appearance of an externally imposed and morally binding force, because of its character of a social regulator of conduct. It assumes the peculiar character of a " moral " force : we do not have to act rightly, but we " ought " to do so.

Morality consists of certain standards and principles of conduct, and says that certain things ought to be done and other things ought not to be done, irrespective of whether individuals want to do them or not, or actually do them or not. The whole sense of moral terms, like " good ", " bad ", " ought ", and so on, is contained in the assertion of standards which do not depend on the particular desires, impulses and actions of individuals. And such standards come to be conceived, and necessarily come to be conceived, precisely because of the social necessity of regulating individual conduct.

Of course, it is one thing to conceive and recognise such standards and another thing to operate them. Generally speaking, every society evolves various forms of sanctions to teach and persuade people to do what they ought, ranging from mild praise or blame to systems of reward and punishment—the latter, however, being mostly reserved for actions directly involving security of life or property. But in societies containing class antagonisms, and where people profit at others' expense and compete with one another, a large part of morality invariably assumes the form of something which is preached to others but which one tries to evade oneself. Morality is inseparable from hypocrisy. Finally, when moral standards are not merely often evaded but are placed in doubt and ignored altogether, and when the various moral sanctions vacillate and weaken, that is one sign that the social system concerned is breaking up and changing.

The whole of social intercourse is conditioned by and based on the production relations of society. And so morality, as a regulator of social intercourse, is in every society the product of definite production relations. It reflects them and changes with them, and each class in society evolves its own moral ideas corresponding to its peculiar class position.

" Men consciously or unconsciously derive their moral ideas in the last resort from the practical relations on which their class position is based," wrote Engels, " from the economic relations in which they carry on production and exchange. . . . All former moral theories are the product, in the last analysis, of the economic stage which society had reached at the particular epoch."[1]

This being so, it is natural that moral ideas should in many ways differ as between different social systems and different classes. At the same time, we should expect to find, as we do find, that there is always something, and often a great deal, in common between them. For the different social systems and classes represent " different stages of the same historical development and have therefore a common historical background, and for that reason alone they necessarily have much in common. Even more. In similar or approximately similar stages of economic development moral theories must of necessity be more or less in agreement." For example, " from the moment when private property in movable objects developed, in all societies in which this property existed there must be this moral law in common : Thou shalt not steal."[2]

The ethics of any social group is the expression of the concrete nature of their freedom and their aspirations for freedom—which has its basis in the place they occupy in social production and their relationship to the means of production. In so far as such a group may remain under the influence and sway of some other group, they may accept the moral ideas of that other group—often to their own detriment and to the advantage of the other, since it serves to keep them in subjection. But in so far as they become conscious of and begin to struggle for their own aims, begin to play an active and not merely a passive part in the process of social change, begin to assert their own freedom, they develop their own morality in the process.

Why does freedom entail morals ? It is because freedom in action is the very opposite of acting on impulse or because of

---

[1] Engels *Anti-Duhring*, Part 1, ch. 9.   [2] *Ibid.*

external compulsion. In so far as people act on impulse or because of external compulsion, they are the very reverse of free but are constrained by chance or external causes. People act freely when they themselves, deliberately and knowingly, determine their course of action. Hence in realising and exercising their freedom people create their maxims or principles of action, which constitute their moral ideas. Their morals then correspond to the conditions and aims of their struggle, as determined on the basis of their actual conditions of material life. At the same time, they create institutions and social sanctions which, in this respect, serve as the external embodiment and defence of their morals and of the kind and degree of freedom of action which they have attained or are striving for.

The modern working class, for example, has created, and is creating, its own morality, which receives particular expression in such institutions as the trade union movement and the Communist Party—a morality of solidarity and of mutual assistance, and of putting the common struggle before the particular and short-term interests of the individual. Bourgeois morality differs from this in many ways. If many working people remain under the influence of bourgeois morality—or what this often comes to today, bourgeois lack of morality—that simply means that they remain relatively passive slaves of the capitalist system, although they may themselves think and be assured by their employers that they are behaving with great strength of mind and independence.

Thus if a worker urged to take part in his trade union struggle replies that he will not do so because everyone should look after himself, that simply means that he has imbibed the individualistic elements of bourgeois morality, which have been pumped into him by capitalist propaganda. It also means that he does not in fact know how to look after himself, since the ideas evolved by the capitalists for looking after their own affairs are not suited to the entirely opposite purpose of assisting the workers.

In class-divided society, morality is always and necessarily class morality. It expresses precisely the requirements, the social consciousness and the measure and kind of freedom of the various classes. And when a class is going down, its morality goes down with it, and gives way to a different morality. We can say that that morality is higher which serves to advance society a step further on the road of material progress and freedom. These two things are inseparable, since in struggling for more freedom people realise their material progress, and in struggling for material progress they realise more freedom. To live more fully is the goal of all free and active life, and this alone provides the objective criterion for judging what morality is higher.

At present, no morality is higher than that which is the expression of the class struggle of the working class. If those who bemoan the decline of morals in capitalist society want to find examples of moral principle, this is where they should look. They do not do so because they are both ashamed and frightened.

" Our morality is entirely subordinated to the interests of the class struggle of the proletariat. Our morality is derived from the interests of the class struggle of the proletariat," wrote Lenin. " . . . Morality is what serves to destroy the old, exploiting society and to unite all the toilers around the proletariat, which is building up a new, communist society. Communist morality is the morality which serves this struggle, which unites the toilers. . . ."[1]

When class antagonisms are abolished in socialist and communist society, then morality does become human and not class morality.

" As society has hitherto moved in class antagonism, morality was always a class morality ", wrote Engels. " It has either justified the domination and the interests of the ruling class, or, as soon as the oppressed class has become powerful enough, it has represented the revolt against this domination and the future interests of the oppressed. That in this process there has on the whole been progress in morality . . . cannot be doubted. But we have not yet passed beyond class morality. A

[1] Lenin, *The Tasks of the Youth Leagues.*

really human morality which transcends class antagonisms and their legacies in thought becomes possible only at a stage of society which has not only overcome class contradictions but has even forgotten them in practical life."[1]

Such morality expresses the principles and maxims of free action in " an association in which the free development of each is the condition for the free development of all".[2] It is deduced from nothing else than knowledge of human requirements and of how to satisfy them. And in conditions where people have deliberate, conscious control over the means of satisfying their requirements, it is the expression of their freedom and the principle guiding their free activities. The ethics of the freedom struggle of the working class, which does not reject but incorporates all that is positive and durable in the whole moral evolution of mankind, prepares the way and lays the basis.

Although human morality does not yet exist, we can perhaps guess at some of its characteristics. It is not dogmatic, but scientific and self-critical. It does not encourage self-righteousness and moral spluttering and frothing, but is calm and reasonable. For it, immoral behaviour is simply anti-social behaviour due to weakness and lack of education, and its aim is not to punish but to reform and educate. It is in all respects kind and humane, and values above everything else the free development and happiness of the human individual.

We can conclude that if we should oppose the philosophy which says that morals are decreed by heaven, we should also oppose the philosophy, no less common today in bourgeois circles, which says that judgments of good and bad are simply expressions of emotional attitudes and can have no basis in reality. If socialists are asked, why do you consider this good and that bad, they need neither preach sermons nor shrug their shoulders. Socialist morality is founded on appreciation of the real conditions and real requirements of the actual freedom struggle of mankind.

[1] Engels, loc. cit.
[2] Marx and Engels, Manifesto of the Communist Party, ch. 2.

CONCLUSION

WE have now completed this survey of the fundamental ideas of Marxist philosophy, having in the three volumes considered materialism and the dialectical method, the materialist conception of history, and the theory of knowledge. What we have been considering are simply the fundamental ideas which Marxism has worked out and established by scientific study and practical application not as a completed and dogmatic system but as a basis and a beginning. The whole point of these ideas is that they should be used and applied and creatively developed in scientifically posing and solving the many theoretical and practical problems of our time.

Ours is the time when people are not only immeasurably extending their mastery over nature but also establishing their mastery over their own social organisation. The outcome will be that people themselves, by their own conscious and collective decisions, will control their own lives, fully understand their own requirements, and go ahead to satisfy them. Marxist ideas, because they are drawn from the total scientific and social achievements of humanity, help us to tackle the problems which arise in this process. They are the ideas to guide and serve in building communist society—that is to say, in realising truly human conditions of existence. And so they represent a permanent achievement for humanity. There is every reason to think that, with further scientific and social advance, the creative use of Marxist ideas and their further development will bring them ever closer to reality and make them ever more effective instruments for the progress of mankind.

But the future has to be fought for. And having completed this survey, we will conclude by considering some of the problems which confront us in that fight.

The ideological superstructure of society always reflects the economic basis. And so in general, periods when a new basis is rising and forming are periods of cultural achievements—of new ideas and discoveries in all spheres, expressing the achievements, aspirations and self-confidence of new, rising classes. But when the old basis is decaying and its defenders are desperately striving to maintain it in existence, there occur periods of decay and disintegration in ideas and culture.

It is natural, therefore, that the general crisis of capitalism should be reflected in a general crisis of capitalist culture—in confusion, decay and despair in all fields of ideas and cultural activity. This general crisis is not one of the temporary economic crises of capitalism, which have only secondary and temporary effects in culture, but is a permanent crisis of the whole system, representing the death throes of the system.

At the same time, the present period is not a period of degeneration, because above all it is a period of great progress, the greatest in the history of humanity. For the elements of the new society are coming into being, the struggle is on between the new and the old, and the new society has definitely and irrevocably established itself in the socialist part of the world. It is a period of intense struggle. And so the state of confusion and decay into which capitalist culture has entered is, on its part, by no means a passive state. In general, the ideological superstructure always actively serves its basis, and today this activity is very marked indeed and has become a feverish effort by all and any means to preserve the dying system and to stave off the advance of socialism.

An important feature of the general crisis of capitalism is that the capitalist class is driven to turn back upon and to begin to undermine and destroy its own past achievements.

Thus, for example, the capitalist class used to stand for democracy but is now turning against it. Originally, the bourgeoisie fought for democracy against feudal rule, because it was by means of democratic institutions that they could best take power from the former rulers and become the rulers themselves. And then they were able to concede democratic gains won by the working class, because capitalism was still advancing and was able to influence the working class within the democratic system. But now, in the period of monopoly capitalism, democratic institutions are becoming a hindrance and a danger to the undisputed rule of the monopolists. Hence the recurrent endeavours to undermine democratic rights and to replace democratic government by fascist violence.

Again, the capitalist class used to stand for national dignity and independence but is now turning against it. The modern monopoly capitalists not only trample on the rights of other nations but betray the vital interests of their own nation, all for the sake of their own profits.

Although the apologists of capitalism try to make out that they are casting off old prejudices in order to embrace new ideas, this turning against and betrayal of everything positive with which it used to be associated remains characteristic of all the capitalist class now does. And this applies equally in the sphere of ideas and culture, in the sciences, philosophy and the arts.

In art and literature, for example, there is a retreat from realism. The task of the profound portrayal and criticism of reality has fallen into disfavour. In the sciences, the humanistic task of increasing knowledge for the increase of men's collective power and welfare has given place to the wholesale perversion of science for militaristic purposes. In philosophy the capitalist world has passed from optimism to pessimism, from the idea that we can gain ever increasing knowledge of reality to the idea that such knowledge is impossible, from the idea that we can improve our conditions of life to the idea that progress is an illusion, and from the lay tradition of free inquiry and criticism to clericalism, authority and dogma. The clerics and obscurantists, who were formerly on the defensive, are now on the offensive, taking advantage of the fact that their former opponents have announced that reason is helpless. So-called professional philosophy is left without life or spirit; and the dying scholasticism of the late Middle Ages, which had degenerated into petty quibbling and hair-splitting, was a fertile garden compared with the barrenness and futility of contemporary bourgeois philosophy. In the journals of the professional bourgeois philosophers today such traits have been magnified a thousand times, and have become their substitute for any positive inquiry. Their philosophies, turning back on all past achievements, offer no solution whatever to any of the practical or theoretical problems facing mankind.

The task of the working class movement, in leading the way to end the old society and build a new one, is also to defend all the positive achievements of the old society. The capitalist class itself is turning against everything progressive which mankind owes to the capitalist epoch. Our task is to take charge of that heritage, and to secure it as part of the building materials of the future—to defend all the achievements of human culture, to build on them and carry them forward.

If, then, the preservation and future of culture, as of all civilisation, is in the hands of the working class, it follows that a working class leadership worthy of the name cannot but take a responsible attitude in relation to cultural questions, as to political and economic questions. The working class party necessarily has a policy, a " party line ", in relation to cultural questions.

In defending our heritage from the past, our task is always to carry it on to a new and higher stage.

Defending democratic institutions and democratic rights, for example, requires the building of a very broad popular alliance, which lays the basis for a higher form of democracy, namely, people's democracy.

Defending our national independence and national sovereignty, we must advance from narrow bourgeois nationalism to socialist internationalism, which recognises the equal rights of all nations and establishes the rights of each on the basis of equality and friendship between all.

Defending the heritage of realism in art and literature, we develop the new, socialist realism, which more truly reflects the many-sidedness and power of human individuals and of human association.

Defending the heritage of science, of free inquiry and the

humanist tradition, we carry scientific discovery forward and free the sciences from the shackles of monopolist control and bourgeois ideology.

Defending the heritage of philosophy, as the striving to understand the world and man's place and destiny in it, we overcome the old metaphysical and idealist notions in philosophy and carry it forward to a new, scientific stage, firmly based on the sciences, illumining our problems and showing the way ahead.

The dual task of defending and carrying forward applies, in fact, in every sphere of the working class struggle. In relation to industrial struggles, for example, we uphold the foundation principles of the trade unions and carry them forward in the battle for socialism, and we uphold the old Labour aim of nationalisation of industry and carry it forward to socialist nationalisation.

We have this task in *all* spheres of economic, political and cultural life, because our task is to change the world and create really human conditions of life, which involves a struggle in the arts, the sciences and philosophy, as well as in economics and politics. Or we may say that working class politics, the struggle of the working class to win power and to build socialism, embraces *every* aspect of social life.

One of the chief manifestations of capitalist influence in the working class movement is the idea that the working class movement does not need philosophy and culture, is not capable of developing them, but may accept scraps of them at second hand from the so-called educated classes. Yet has the working class no interest in such matters ? On the contrary, the whole progressive heritage of humanity belongs to the working people, who must prepare to take it over. The working people will conquer the world. And hence everything in the world and everything that mankind has discovered or created, from the smallest particle in the atom up to the heights of culture, is the concern of the working people. Hence they have to create, and are creating, thousands, and hundreds of thousands and millions of new cadres of fighters, who are thoroughly equipped not only with militancy and practical experience but with wide knowledge and culture.

The old social system of exploitation of man by man, the old culture of the exploiting classes, was directed by the tiny minority of exploiters and shaped by them to serve their purposes. But they could never have achieved anything if they had not been sustained by the efforts and toil of the working masses. And now their day is over. The new social system and the new culture is being created and directed by the working people themselves, whose labour has always been the mainspring of social life, and will far surpass the old. Our philosophy equips us to fight capitalism and its ideologies, to take over power, and to build the happy and glorious socialist future.

BIBLIOGRAPHY

The following are the principal sources in classical Marxist writings dealing with problems of the theory of knowledge which have been consulted and quoted in this volume :—

MARX :

> *Capital*
> *Critique of Political Economy*, Preface
> *The Poverty of Philosophy*
> *Economic-Philosophical Manuscripts*

MARX AND ENGELS :

> *The German Ideology*
> *Correspondence*

ENGELS :

> *Anti-Duhring*
> *Ludwig Feuerbach*
> *Socialism, Utopian and Scientific*, Introduction
> *Dialectics of Nature*

LENIN :

> *Materialism and Empirio-Criticism*
> *Karl Marx*
> *Tasks of the Youth Leagues*
> *Philosophical Notebooks*

STALIN :

> *Dialectical and Historical Materialism*
> *Anarchism or Socialism ?*
> *Concerning Marxism in Linguistics*
> *Economic Problems of Socialism in the U.S.S.R.*

MAO :

> *On Practice*

INDEX